AD\

"Consumer expectations of privacy and government regulations are reshaping the way advertisers approach their day-to-day work. The InfoTrust team provides insight into the new marketing reality and actionable steps readers can take to be more successful today."

—KEVIN HARTMAN, CHIEF ANALYTICS EVANGELIST AT GOOGLE

"The fear of the unknown can be paralyzing for a business and their partners, but as the InfoTrust team illustrates, the unknown can be an opportunity (and advantage) for those who mindfully plan ahead."

—JON EUERLE, MEASUREMENT PRODUCT MANAGER, ENTERPRISE DIGITAL CAPABILITIES AT GENERAL MILLS

"Long, Loban, Oldham, and Yastrebenetsky combine their diverse professional experiences to help enterprise organizations understand where to start when it comes to privacy, as well as a road map for maturing their own expertise in the space. A must-read for all marketers going forward to understand the dos and don'ts of personal data collection."

—CAROLINE BASYN, STRATEGY & TRANSFORMATION EUROPE AT PEPSICO

"As privacy moves to the forefront of marketers' minds, this book serves as an excellent blueprint for those attempting to navigate increasingly complicated data collection waters."

—SOUMYADEB MITRA, FOUNDER & CEO AT RUDDERSTACK

"The marketing landscape continues to change dramatically as data privacy takes its rightful place in the public's consciousness. Crawl, Walk, Run helps craft the path forward for the enlightened marketer and publisher to evolve."

—ADAM SYMSON, PRESIDENT, CHIEF EXECUTIVE OFFICER AT THE E.W. SCRIPPS COMPANY

"With shifting expectations around consumer data and privacy legislation, marketers are actively rethinking how they approach their data collection strategies. Michael Loban and team provide a detailed look at this new privacy-centric landscape and provide useable recommendations that can be followed by senior executives today."

—PETER FADER, PROFESSOR OF MARKETING AT THE WHARTON SCHOOL, UNIVERSITY OF PENNSYLVANIA, CO-FOUNDER AND DIRECTOR OF THETA, AND CO-AUTHOR OF *THE CUSTOMER-BASE AUDIT*

"After simplifying the extremely technical aspects of Google Marketing Platform in their last Crawl, Walk, Run book, the InfoTrust team has done it again, helping marketers to better understand the privacy-related challenges (and solutions) that lie ahead."

—FD WILDER, SENIOR ADVISOR AT MCKINSEY & COMPANY AND ADJUNCT FACULTY (EXEC ED) AT HARVARD BUSINESS SCHOOL

"The InfoTrust team goes well beyond simple consumer privacy compliance in their newest Crawl, Walk, Run book, enabling advertisers to craft a durable first-party data strategy that can power marketing engines well into the future. While their first book is a must-read (and is currently sitting on my desk), this book goes even further and is all the more relevant today as privacy-related legislation and corporate actions change the competitive landscape."

—DANIEL MCCARTHY, ASSISTANT PROFESSOR OF MARKETING AT EMORY UNIVERSITY'S GOIZUETA BUSINESS SCHOOL AND CO-FOUNDER AT THETA

BECOMING A PRIVACY-CENTRIC MARKETING ORGANIZATION

PART OF THE BESTSELLING
CRAWL, WALK, RUN SERIES

BECOMING A **PRIVACY-CENTRIC** MARKETING ORGANIZATION

LUCAS LONG
MICHAEL LOBAN
ALEX YASTREBENETSKY
KENT OLDHAM

LIONCREST
PUBLISHING

BECOMING A PRIVACY-CENTRIC MARKETING ORGANIZATION

FIRST EDITION

ISBN 978-1-5445-3963-8 *Hardcover*
978-1-5445-3962-1 *Paperback*
978-1-5445-3961-4 *Ebook*

At InfoTrust, we champion a culture of experimentation in the face of the new privacy-centric reality. By fearlessly testing new marketing strategies, you can future-proof your organization. In the spirit of practicing what we preach, we present our very own Crawl, Walk, Run: Becoming a Privacy-Centric Marketing Organization NFT. To access it, use the QR code below.

CONTENTS

DISCLAIMER

The information covered in this book is not intended to be legal advice or counsel. You should not act or refrain from acting on the basis of any content included in this book regarding legal compliance without obtaining appropriate legal guidance. The contents of this book contain general information related to various laws and regulations, but may not reflect your current situation. In addition, applicable laws and regulations regularly change. This is particularly true with respect to data privacy laws and regulations. Therefore, any laws and regulations described or otherwise referenced in this book may not be current when you read the book or even at the time of publication. We disclaim all liability for actions you take or fail to take based on anything in this book. Any action you take or any action you refrain from taking based on the information in this book is entirely at your own discretion and risk.

INTRODUCTION

THE PRIVACY-CENTRIC REALITY

On December 31, 2019, a marketer at an enterprise company in California could do (nearly) whatever they wanted with consumer data. Their only real limitation was their own imagination. A marketer could monitor a user's activity across any website and could even follow them across the internet, using cookies to identify and target them with ads for their product. They could buy and sell user data to third parties for profit or analysis. All this, without needing to ask for user consent or provide the option to opt out. Most consumers had no idea that their data was valuable, let alone actively bought and sold without their knowledge. It was the wild west of data collection, and nearly every organization big and small was capitalizing.

That is, until the next morning.

When that same marketer awoke on January 1, 2020, their job was much more difficult than the day before. The California Consumer Privacy Act (CCPA) officially went into effect, changing marketing in the state overnight. Suddenly, large organizations had to disclose to their California-based users whether they were selling their information. And if so, they had to disclose what information was being sold to whom, and how it was used. Further, they had to give them the choice to opt out, meaning users could choose not to allow their data to be sold. And if that wasn't complicated enough, a California-based user could now ask for access to their data history—a request that seemed simple enough on the surface but proved to be a logistical nightmare.

The CCPA affects most advertisers at large organizations who market to consumers in California, regardless of where the company is based—which means it impacts a great deal of organizations. However, it's just one of many similar regulations across the globe that have put marketers in a tricky position: fail to comply and risk tarnishing the organization's reputation or comply and explain to upper management why their strategy is no longer effective.

Many marketers have come to us at InfoTrust looking for advice. As a privacy-centric digital analytics company, these marketers are hoping we have a few tricks up our sleeves to help them maneuver around compliance issues. When we tell them that these regulations aren't going away and that the best move is to become compliant, they explain that they feel that their hands are tied between expectations of the organization to produce results and legal requirements.

But for those who continue with the status quo, it won't be long before the danger of non-compliance outweighs the benefits.

In late August of 2022, a global beauty retailer continued to sell users' personal information past the compliance date issued by the CCPA. Not only did this company fail to give the user the option to opt out, but they even failed to inform users they were collecting and selling their data at all. The California Attorney General gave the organization 30 days to become compliant. They chose not to do so.[1]

In response, the state of California slapped them with a $1.2 million fine. But for a company worth $10 billion, the money wasn't the issue. You can make an argument that from an advertising standpoint, $1.2 million is a small price to pay for the targeting enhancements gained with customer data. The real problem is that the company made headlines for nearly six weeks after the incident.

Consider the fine just the tip of the iceberg. Below the surface, there is first the cost to become compliant. Based on how close to compliance the organization may or may not be, this can be a considerable investment. Then there is the cost of responding to the incident. Depending on how much media attention the upset has caused, this can become expensive. Finally, there is the loss of revenue from brand equity damage. While the total impact for this particular organization is yet to be seen (as we write this book in the fourth quarter of 2022), they are now in the unfortunate position of finding out just how much consumers care about their privacy. It's safe to assume that after the media picked up the story, the entire marketing department was working overtime to find a solution.

In a 2021 study by Adobe, two-thirds of respondents said that

---

1 Lucas Long, "U.S. Privacy Enforcement Heats Up: 1.2 Million Reasons to Respect Privacy Rights," InfoTrust, August 25, 2022, https://infotrust.com/articles/u-s-privacy-enforcement-heats-up-1-2-million-reasons-to-respect-privacy-rights/.

they would stop buying from brands that misused their data.[2] Granted, people often overstate their intentions in surveys like this. The actual fallout could be less. But this theory is proven again and again every time a negative story is linked to an organization.

Just how costly consumer data non-compliance could be in the future is unknown. When making decisions around compliance (or willful non-compliance), take time to consider your organization's risk tolerance when it comes to bad PR and multimillion-dollar fines.

If your organization is still non-compliant (or if you have no clue whether you are or not), know you aren't alone. Many large companies still rely on third-party data. And as state and national governments crack down on violations, we'll likely see more and more companies navigating the fallout caused by ignoring legal requirements.

WHO WE ARE AND WHAT WE DO

InfoTrust has spent more than a decade in the digital space as a consulting firm in digital analytics and data privacy. We've seen the good, the bad, and the ugly when it comes to consumer data acquisition, compliance, and use. We know what organizations need and we also understand what consumers demand.

Our specific insight comes at a time when a confluence of skills is necessary to revamp your data strategy. Some organizations work with legal teams. Others specialize in data. Many operate

---

2 Adobe Communications Team, "7 in 10 Customers Will Buy More from Brands They Trust; Abandon Those They Don't," *Adobe Experience Cloud Blog*, November 4, 2021, https://business.adobe.com/uk/blog/perspectives/7-in-10-customers-will-buy-more-from-brands-they-trust-uk.

in media. But over the last ten years, we've positioned ourselves at the intersection of all three, right when organizations need that specialty.

We are the largest independent Google Marketing Platform Sales Partner in our industry of analytics services. We work closely with Google to publish content on martech stack durability and privacy-centric marketing. We also host and participate in events and summits that feature digital analytics and privacy thought leaders from our team at InfoTrust, Google, and some of the world's most recognizable brands.

We're a consulting firm in digital analytics, but we've also built a product that brings visibility to data being collected on digital properties. During development of Tag Inspector—our proprietary tag auditing and monitoring platform—we worked closely with compliance and legal teams. You'd be hard pressed to find anyone else on the planet that has analyzed more data collection architectures than our team.

This book is authored by four of us, all members of the InfoTrust team, including the Chief Executive Officer and co-founder Alex Yastrebenetsky, Chief Growth Officer and co-founder Michael Loban, Director of Privacy Strategy Lucas Long, and Chief Operating Officer Kent Oldham. In addition to hearing directly from us, you'll hear from trusted members of our team. We proudly feature our colleagues' biographies at the beginning of a handful of chapters. Read them to find out why each contributor is at the forefront of data strategy and is distinguished in their respective field.

To get the most out of this book, check out our privacy-centric marketing enablement portal. The portal isn't merely additional information on data strategy—it's your ticket into our world. It's updated with the most current information curated by our incredible team. It includes industry-specific advice on location-dependent regulations and on building durable first-party data strategies. The Portal unlocks free access to hyper-relevant content that we simply can't include in this book. Access it while you read and remember to check back periodically to stay ahead in your market.

Use the QR code to access the portal.

As a marketer, you are in an extremely tough position. Losing access to insight from third-party data is truly a major disruption in marketing. But the wonderful thing about disruption is that for those who are willing to adapt, it can be a moment of true innovation.

This moment of disruption allows organizations to leverage new privacy standards to gain a competitive advantage in their marketplace. Updating your data collection strategy doesn't have to negatively impact the bottom line. For those that are willing to test, refine, and explore new possibilities, the new world of data privacy can be an incredible opportunity.

Whether your organization simply needs to become compliant or you want to leverage your data strategy as an integral part of your business plan, this is your guide to win in the privacy-centric reality.

CHAPTER ONE

THE NEW WORLD OF DATA PRIVACY

In 2017, the InfoTrust team had just started outlining a significant project with a global organization. Midway through the project proposal, new data privacy regulations were put into place in 2018. We were expecting these changes, but our client wasn't. Concerned by all the media attention over the new regulations around consent and persistent tracking, our client pumped the brakes on the entire project.

"This needs to be cleared through our privacy team," explained the executive. We were surprised, considering that we specialize in privacy-centric data strategy.

"Do you know what they're specifically looking for?" we asked.

"We don't know," the executive said. "But they still need to approve it."

We agreed that it wouldn't be a problem and that we'd happily walk the privacy team through our proposal.

The proposal made its way through their data privacy team and landed on the desk of the legal department. The legal team read the document and agreed the project scope would be compliant, but they weren't completely confident in how the new regulations would impact the company. They asked to sleep on it.

Meanwhile, the business stakeholders constantly notified us. They were anxious about the extended timeline. They were worried the funds would be lost for the project if work didn't begin soon. That's when we got another call from the executive.

"Our new chief information officer has more documents that you need to sign from a data processing standpoint."

"Send them over ASAP," we replied.

They did include a privacy impact assessment, but much of what was sent didn't apply to us or the project. We were left holding a bunch of documents that someone unfamiliar with the project decided were important but were actually irrelevant. To make matters even more complicated, the client's internal legal team knew they needed to approve the project, but they weren't yet familiar with the new legal landscape. It was taking time for them to catch up. Meanwhile, other members in the organization were growing frustrated because the timeline continued to be delayed.

The business needed the project to go through not just because the budget was set aside, but because without it they couldn't measure the effectiveness of various campaigns on their websites. The siloed nature of their sites created a massive blind spot in their data, which had serious downstream implications and made it particularly difficult to become compliant with government privacy laws. The business knew they needed to act fast, yet lack of certainty created a hot potato situation, with everyone tossing the data privacy strategy to someone further down the line.

Three months into this debacle, we still did not have the green light; at the end of the fiscal year, they lost the budget.

This story illustrates the impact of new data privacy laws that are popping up across the US and globally. They are leaving entire organizations just as paralyzed as our client was. Internally, *no one wants to be the person who drops the ball*, so companies around the world are currently stuck in a holding pattern.

If you haven't already begun to incorporate a privacy-centric data strategy in your organization, brace yourself for impact. As new regulations continue to come into play, your organization's marketing department will be forced to halt business as usual without a plan to restart in place. The only surefire way to keep your business on track is to completely renovate your data collection strategy.

Adherence to new regulations is urgent, but we aren't suggesting that you sprint out of the gate. There isn't a quick fix to data privacy, and that means it will take time for your organization to first become compliant, and then focus on a long-term data strategy. That's why this book is part of our best-selling series, *Crawl, Walk, Run*. Before you can run, you must learn to crawl. This book is your guide to preparing for the race. Once you start, you choose how you will compete.

THE COOKIE JAR IS CRACKING

If this new reality feels daunting, you're not alone. According to a 2019 study by Gartner Research, almost one out of five marketers report privacy compliance as their main concern across marketing channels.[3] Nearly two-thirds—73 percent—of marketers fear that privacy concerns will negatively impact their ability to sell.[4]

As a marketer, you're already feeling the impact of greater privacy demands. Historically, we've relied on cookies to give us unprecedented, precise insight into what consumers are doing online. This incredible piece of tech enabled so much more insight about consumer preference than we could ever deduce from customer feedback or in-store behavior.

Cookies are small text files placed on a user's browser. They save small amounts of information for later reference. For advertising use cases, the information saved is often a unique identifier, used to track the user across interactions and websites.

There are two types of cookies. First-party cookies are created from and only readable from the domain/URL/website that a user is on. Third-party cookies are created and readable from a domain that is not the principal domain (in other words, not the domain that is currently in the browser bar).

Tags are JavaScript that runs on the page and are the technical mechanism via which cookies are set and read from, as well as the mechanism that collects data.

---

3 Joseph Enever and Evan Neufeld, "Survey Analysis: Postcompliance Marketing Privacy Challenges and Opportunities," Gartner, July 18, 2019, https://www.gartner.com/en/documents/3950434.

4 Anna Maria Virzi and Lizzy Foo Kune, "Presentation of Marketing Data and Analytics Survey 2018: Messy Data and Mismatched Resources Undermine Analytics Teams," Gartner, July 19, 2018, https://www.gartner.com/en/documents/3883173.

But now that third-party cookies are soon-to-be outdated, cross-domain activities like retargeting—at least in the way we know it today—will disappear. For one, Google Chrome joined a list of other online browsers to ditch third-party cookies by the end of 2024.[5] Meanwhile, other internet browsers like Apple's Safari and technology like ad blockers are making it more difficult to target ads across the digital domain.

Changes in technology aren't the only thing altering the way we collect and use data. Evolving government regulations, like the one from the opening story, include strict data privacy requirements with serious penalties. For example, the European Union's General Data Protection Regulation (GDPR) now requires "the right to be forgotten" and "explicit consent," or an affirmative, unambiguous indication to process personal data. Break the rules and your business could face fines of up to 4 percent of annual revenue.[6] Brazil, China, and Thailand have also created new regulations, with most countries on the horizon. The United States is catching up policy-wise, with California leading the pack by requiring businesses to stop targeted advertising to users upon their request.

Those are just a few examples of how tech and government are redefining marketing. Considering that more countries and states are continuously updating their privacy laws with stricter policies, it's reasonable to assume that this trend will continue across the globe and into the future.

---

5 Jennifer Elias, "Google Delays Cookie-Cutting to 2024," *CNBC*, July 27, 2022, https://www.cnbc.com/2022/07/27/google-delays-cookie-cutting-to-2024.html.

6 European Parliament and the Council of the European Union, "Regulation (EU) 2016/679 of the European Parliament and of the of 27 April 2016 on the Protection of Natural Persons with Regard to the Processing of Personal Data and on the Free Movement of Such Data, and Repealing Directive 95/46/EC (General Data Protection Regulation)," *Official Journal of the European Union*, no. L119 (2016): 1–88, https://eur-lex.europa.eu/legal-content/EN/TXT/PDF/?uri=CELEX:32016R0679.

The future is privacy-centric.

HOW WE GOT HERE

This book is the key to winning in what we are calling the privacy-centric reality. To truly understand the future of marketing, it's worth examining the past. Where did unfettered access to all that personal data lead us?

In 2016, the InfoTrust team traveled from Cincinnati to Dubai to speak at a conference on analytics strategy. During a long layover, a few of us tried to log on to the airport's Wi-Fi. Before we could use it, we had to enter some personal data, like name, age, gender, and zip code. It was a tedious process, as the landing page was in a foreign language.

Are they asking for my zip code or address? First name or email?

If you've ever been in a similar position, all that fiddling around might have given you a lot of time to wonder: *Why do they even want this information?*

Really—why does the airport want to know so much about us?

And what do they actually do with all that data?

While presenting at the event, one of the fellow panelists shed light on this question.

"What kind of consumer data should my organization collect?" asked a marketer in the audience.

"All of it!" the panelist answered confidently.

His reasoning? Data collection is easy, storage is cheap, and consumers are willing to give up just about anything you ask for. You can figure out what to do with all that information later.

The panelist's views represent how marketers historically approached data acquisition. Six years ago data collection was easy and cheap, and customers weren't asking why it was obtained, where it was stored, or how it was used.

But once consumers started seeing ads for the odd thing they'd searched for the week before, they grew suspicious. Eventually consumers started to wonder what companies were doing with all that data and whether the product or service they received in return was really worth it.

Is twenty minutes of slow internet at the airport a fair exchange for your personal data?

© marketoonist.com

As an individual, your answer to that question represents a fascinating historical moment. As a marketer...it's totally irrelevant. What really matters is what the consumer believes, and consumers around the world no longer think it's fair for companies to access so much of their personal data without something in return.

So what does this mean for *you*?

THREE PRIVACY-CENTRIC FORCES

We've identified three elemental forces driving better privacy strategies. Understand how all three relate to your specific organization, and you'll be able to build a winning privacy strategy. These three forces include consumer expectations, technology changes, and government regulations.

Surprisingly, it's not the regulations and tech that are driving this monumental shift (although it can feel that way sometimes). The massive force that's redefined marketing is the same force that always shapes this industry: consumer expectations. That's where we'll begin.

CONSUMER EXPECTATIONS

As a marketer, you've probably understood for a long time how consumer data is collected, used, and stored. You've known that it has immense value and that much of your job revolves around acquiring and deriving insight from that data.

But your consumers are just starting to learn how and why their data is being used.

Many consumers are now learning that their information has been collected from them without their knowledge or consent. They perhaps know that some organizations have misused that data. They may feel confused or upset by that. Simultaneously, they've read in the news or on social media about organizations that have failed to protect that data, exposing their information to bad actors.

© marketoonist.com

Your consumers don't know what's happening to the degree that you do. But many do know that *something* is happening, and they certainly feel some way about it. The degree of the response may change from person to person, but most agree that they care about data privacy and want greater data protection.[7]

How much customers care about data privacy, however, varies. It depends on the target audience, the industry, and what the

7 Cisco, *Cisco 2021 Consumer Privacy Survey: Building Consumer Confidence through Transparency and Control* (June 2021), https://www.cisco.com/c/dam/en_us/about/doing_business/trust-center/docs/cisco-cybersecurity-series-2021-cps.pdf.

organization is doing with the data. Many people feel the value they get from social media is worth their information. But few people would have the same attitude about their financial information from their banking app. Or would consent to an insurance company using Facebook data to increase premiums on their insurance policies.

If consumer expectations vary from person to person and from industry to industry, it makes sense that so too does their response to privacy regulation and compliance. Foreign policy experts and diplomats often use the phrase "virtue of proportionate response," meaning that retaliation shouldn't exceed the initial strike. In the case of consumer data privacy, many don't necessarily know how to respond proportionately because they aren't exactly sure the degree to which they've been impacted. Yet they do know that it was bad enough for governments to get involved.

If you don't know what someone did to you, but everyone says it's bad, it's likely you will respond harshly no matter what truly took place. The point? Don't expect a proportionate response from your consumers without a strategy in place. For example, when confronted with a cookie consent overlay, many will decline all. That means you'll need to be able to gain similar insight using alternative tactics.

At the end of the day, you know your customers best and therefore can best predict how they will respond to your privacy policy. Our aim is to help you first become compliant (as in meeting the minimum bar) and then address consumer expectations around which you can make decisions regarding your data privacy strategy.

TECHNOLOGY CHANGES

Recently, Google Ad Manager ran an experiment where it disabled access to cookies for a small fraction of online users to see whether ad revenues would fall when cookies were not available. They found that ad revenues fell by a whopping 52 percent for the top 500 global publishers, with a median decline of 64.5 percent per publisher.[8]

This research clarifies that any changes browsers make to further protect the privacy of users (like third-party cookie deprecation) will have a significant impact on the marketing and advertising ecosystem. After conducting split testing across global websites for two years, the InfoTrust team has seen that when given an equal-effort choice to opt in or opt out of cookie usage, approximately 40 to 60 percent of users will opt out.

Given that all the top browsers are currently implementing new technical restrictions, marketers can't delay grappling with the effects coming to the industry. No matter which browser your customers use and how lenient it may be for advertisers, the paradigm is shifting.

Browser technical restrictions are meant to put customer privacy at the center. These changes are likely to both help consumers protect their data and cause some pain to advertisers. Across the board, browsers are restricting access to personal identifiers. According to Meta's narrative, the changes that Apple is introducing on Safari will impact the ability to do personalized

---

8 Deepak Ravichandran and Nitish Korula, *Effect of Disabling Third-Party Cookies on Publisher Revenue*, Google, August 27, 2019, https://services.google.com/fh/files/misc/disabling_third-party_cookies_publisher_revenue.pdf.

advertising to the degree that a small local gym won't be able to successfully carry out an advertising campaign.[9]

But is it really that dire? The truth is that we don't yet know the outcome of cookie deprecation. Certainly it means businesses large and small will be forced to adapt, for better or worse. But before we can build a smart strategy to increase access to consumer data, we have to explore the ways in which browsers you may currently rely on will restrict access to third-party data. For this section, we'll focus on the big three browsers that hold 90 percent of the market: Chrome, Safari, and Firefox.

Google Chrome

Google Chrome is the most widely used browser in the market with a 65.9 percent market share, and therefore will likely impact the largest percent of your users. Chrome doesn't currently have any impactful tracking protecting initiatives, but it does intend to phase out third-party cookies in 2024 alongside its Privacy Sandbox initiative.[10]

In engineering, a "sandbox" is a protected environment. It creates a secure way to run applications, access data, create code, and more without making a mess elsewhere. In this context, it allows the personal information of the user to be accessed without compromising the user's data.

Google's Privacy Sandbox is a set of new functionalities in Chrome to satisfy common advertising and measurement use

9 Dan Levy, "Speaking Up for Small Businesses," Meta, December 16, 2020, https://about.fb.com/news/2020/12/speaking-up-for-small-businesses/.

10 Garett Sloane, "Google Postpones Demise of Cookies to 2024," AdAge, July 27, 2022, https://adage.com/article/digital-marketing-ad-tech-news/google-delays-cookies-demise-2024/2424681.

cases that today are reliant on third-party cookies in a more privacy-focused way.[11] Examples of use cases meant to be addressed are retargeting, advertising to a user based upon inferred interests, and impression frequency capping.

Apple

Safari has an 18.6 percent market share (meaning about 20 percent of users use this browser).[12]

As of October 2022, Safari blocks all third-party cookies by default with their Intelligent Tracking Prevention (ITP) initiative. This is a much stronger stance than Chrome, and suggests this browser is more privacy-focused than alternatives. First-party cookies have significant restrictions, too. The maximum time a cookie using JavaScript can stay on a device is seven days. For cookies set via JavaScript when the user is coming from most advertising sources, that expiration is set to twenty-four hours.[13]

Throughout the development of ITP technology, there has been an arms race between developers and marketers, with marketers creating technical work-arounds and Safari responding with updates to close loopholes and enforce the intent of cross-site tracking prevention. For example, Apple introduced app tracking transparency. Any application is required to be very

11 "Topics: The New Privacy Sandbox Proposal for Interest-Based Advertising," Google Ads Help, February 22, 2022, https://support.google.com/google-ads/answer/11899856?hl=en#:~:text=The%20Privacy%20Sandbox%20is%20a,use%20cases%20for%20online%20businesses.

12 "Browser Market Share Worldwide," StatCounter GlobalStats, accessed August 2022, https://gs.statcounter.com/browser-market-share.

13 "Safari Privacy Overview," Apple, November 2019, https://www.apple.com/safari/docs/Safari_White_Paper_Nov_2019.pdf.

transparent about exactly what platforms are collecting what data within their application.

Apps are also required to give the user an explicit consent over whether that application or any of the platforms running within it will have access to the Identifier for Advertisers (IDFA). The IDFA is the equivalent of a third-party cookie ID within a mobile application ecosystem.

Apple is taking it another step further by introducing private relay. Whenever you access a web page or even an application, they obfuscate and change your IP address, sort of like a VPN. The IP address of a user is typically used to get a general geolocation, like when an advertiser wants to target individuals in the Cincinnati area, for example. It's also often used as one piece of a puzzle to generate an identifier for a user.

Apple has also introduced privacy protection for email. Traditionally platforms could install tracking pixels within an email, allowing them to track whether or not someone opened a specific email. Mail privacy blocks the tracker from operating.

The last bit of tech Apple rolled out is called "hide my email," which creates dummy emails for the user. If a user wants to sign up for a loyalty program on five different websites, Apple provides them with a fake email address for each that Apple associates with their account. That way users can still benefit from the loyalty program without all the marketing emails crowding their inbox.

Mozilla Firefox

Although Firefox only has a 3.2 percent adoption rate, it's worth discussing because it has a strong reputation in the privacy space. Firefox introduced its own enhanced tracking prevention (ETP) in August 2020. ETP provides default tracking prevention for what they call "classified domains," using an industry list (disconnect.me) of known trackers. Third-party cookies are blocked for those classified domains. Any data that is associated with that website—even first-party cookies—is cleared from the browser if the user doesn't go to that website again within forty-five days.[14]

The impact of ETP is nearly the same as ITP: third-party cookies are blocked by default. As a result, companies can't retarget or use one-to-one direct targeting. They can't see the user path to purchase, either.

Ad Blockers

Other technologies beyond browsers give anonymity to users. One piece of tech currently upsetting the marketing industry is ad blockers. Typically, this is a plugin or extension that users add to their browser. Ad blockers stop the code that runs ads and/or accesses personal information if it's from a known advertising platform.

Nearly 30 percent of users in the US are using some kind of ad blocker.[15] And as data privacy continues to make headlines, this number could increase. Clearly, consumers are becoming more literate about data privacy and their online information.

---

14 "Latest Firefox Rolls Out Enhanced Tracking Protection 2.0; Blocking Redirect Trackers by Default," *Mozilla* (blog), August 4, 2020, https://blog.mozilla.org/press/2020/08/latest-firefox-rolls-out-enhanced-tracking-protection-2-0-blocking-redirect-trackers-by-default/.

15 "US Ad Blocking User Penetration, by Demographic, 2019 & 2021 (% of Internet User in Each Group)," Insider Intelligence, July 15, 2019, https://www.insiderintelligence.com/chart/230161/us-ad-blocking-user-penetration-by-demographic-2019-2021-of-internet-users-each-group.

The high use of ad blockers paired with the continuous interplay between marketers and updates in browsers suggests that technical work-arounds aren't a legitimate strategy moving forward. This kind of arms race between tech and marketers in the battle over third-party data isn't sustainable. Instead of searching for loopholes, marketers should look for a long-term strategy that will remain relevant no matter what new technical restriction is created next.

Speaking of evolving restrictions, the third force driving our shift to privacy-centricity is government regulations.

GOVERNMENT REGULATIONS

If your organization serves a global audience, you are likely wondering what compliance with government regulations will look like across countries and states. Most countries have some form of privacy legislation in place. Currently, the European Union has the strongest privacy laws under the General Data Protection Regulation (GDPR). The following global map shows the extent of privacy regulation.

Based on this map, you may be envisioning a patchwork of sites, with users from different locations viewing customized pages that look different based on the government policies that impact them. While this kind of customization is possible, it's not exactly practical.

It will be much easier for organizations to comply by designing their data privacy plan around the most stringent regulations. This is particularly true because while we don't know what future regulations will come into play, we do expect them to increase in reach and severity. Of course, there are nuances for every organization. Companies servicing consumers around the world are going to be far more impacted than small, single-market brands.

For the most up-to-date and specific information regarding the regulations that are currently impacting your organization and those that will in the future, navigate to our privacy-centric marketing enablement portal. This free online resource is continually updated by the InfoTrust team. It covers far more than just the latest privacy regulations. Consider the portal your personalized guide to leveraging our privacy guidelines in your industry.

Use the QR code to access the portal.

It isn't our goal to fully explain every regulation. Rather, this is your blueprint to develop your strategy to a point where you can simply hand it to legal for review and approval. However, while you don't need to examine every global regulation, rest assured that we have. And in our research, we realized that every regulation focuses on the same core themes and protections. By understanding the common language of all regulations, the path to winning in a privacy-centric world becomes clear. Success centers on the same basic three principles:

- Respect user privacy
- First-party ownership of first-party data
- Action based on insight and understanding

If you still aren't convinced that decreasing reliance on third-party data and increasing first-party data is a smart move, we have some bad news. This is the state of play. Like it or not, third-party cookies are going out the door. But once you center your advertising and marketing around the three principles above, you'll create an experience where consumers *want* to give you information because they understand the value of what they'll get in return.

HOW TO WIN IN A PRIVACY-CENTRIC REALITY

We want to help you win in a privacy-centric reality, not simply avoid fines. That's why we haven't gotten too far into the weeds concerning government regulations or technological restrictions. The legal and technical landscape is evolving. We're interested in helping your organization succeed in the future, not just catch up to the present.

In this book we'll show you how to create a privacy-centric data strategy that is not only compliant but stays relevant regardless of the next unforeseen regulation and technology change. One that will help your organization stay on track and functional as you update your data strategy. One that reveals how to collect and use data in a privacy-centric way that will allow you to make better decisions for your customers than before. While your competition is clinging to the past, you will position your organization to dominate the new marketing landscape.

We understand that you might not want to reach privacy-centric ideals, but rather want to do what is required while maintaining current revenue and earnings levels. And we get that it's hard to see a way to do that in this unfamiliar environment, when many of the strategies, tactics, and data you've traditionally had access to are no longer there. Our goal is that by the end of this book, you'll have all the tools you need to strengthen your consumers' trust in you, acquire the data required to effectively market to them, and leverage that data to stay profitable.

When we discussed consumer expectations, we suggested that a strong privacy strategy first meet the threshold of government compliance. For some organizations, that will be their ending point. Certainly, not all businesses will become a privacy-first organization like Apple or Firefox, and that's perfectly fine. Our solution allows marketers to tailor their unique privacy needs to the demands of their organizations.

But for other companies, after they first become compliant, they may choose to make consumer privacy a key pillar of differentiation for their organization. Again, the goal is to raise your privacy standards to meet consumer expectations. If they expect very little, then you understand the degree to which you'll adopt these strategies. If their demands are high, then you'll build privacy into your narrative.

The change is here. Consumers expect more privacy. Technologies protect it. And governments demand it. Marketing is in an adapt-or-fail transition. Government regulations, technological advancements, and new consumer expectations can feel like a tidal wave you haven't prepared for. We're already seeing organizations make the wrong moves—and paying a literal price for these decisions. They're looking for loopholes and technological crutches, hoping to find work-arounds so they can continue to collect as much data as possible.

This book isn't about tips or tricks. It's not a list of technical work-arounds. It's not a detailed landscape of the regulations. Instead, it's a lasting data strategy. A smart plan for the new privacy-centric reality can be the catalyst that pushes you and your organization to new heights.

A strong, trust-based relationship with customers is the only path to a sustainable, effective data strategy.

Yes, the landscape has irrevocably changed. And yes, your job and organization will look different in the coming months. But this upset isn't a bad thing. Far from it. Change creates opportunities for those that are willing to leverage disruption. The organizations that will rise to the top are the ones who rapidly embrace the framework in this book.

And for those who worry that their job will never be the same—you're only half right. You're still a marketer, after all. You'll continue to collect, analyze, and use consumer data. We're just going to help you do it better. So let's build a plan that relies on strategies and technology that delivers business outcomes no matter what new, unexpected privacy standards governments create in the future.

CHAPTER TWO

PRINCIPLES OF USER PRIVACY

Data privacy information is a lot like health and dieting resources. There is a ton of advice out there, but not all of it is dependable. You might find yourself asking questions like:

- Is this accurate?
- What's their agenda?
- This contradicts something else I've seen. Which one is right?

With the prolific and extensive nature of information on this topic, it's easy to get overwhelmed when presented with it all at once. That's why fear-mongering articles like "Google Analytics Is Dead!" are titled in ways to attract (and scare) readers as new developments occur.

When you look at each new data privacy regulation piecemeal, it's overwhelming. It's also ineffective. Trying to follow every new regulation that comes out in every region of your market isn't a good use of time when the landscape isn't static.

But it doesn't need to be so complicated. In reality, the goal is still the same. Marketers are still trying to have a better relationship and understanding of their consumers. The way in which they build those relationships may change, but the result won't be much different than what we see today.

Our system uses a comprehensive approach that outlines the evergreen fundamentals while allowing for local tweaks to address market-level regulatory nuances. Doing so ensures you can cover all your bases easily so that you're always compliant and doing what's best for your business.

PRINCIPLE ONE: RESPECT THE RIGHTS OF USERS

The first principle of a privacy-centric marketing strategy is to respect users and their data. This idea of respect is the bedrock of privacy. It's closely related to the idea of fairness and an equal value exchange that we discussed in the last chapter—if you respect your customer's privacy, you will be in a better position to create a value exchange they will agree to.

FAIR VALUE PROPOSITION

The problem for organizations who do not put privacy at the forefront of their data strategy is one of value. In the airport example, the perceived value of customer data (and the time to input it) outweighed the perceived value of slow internet. To put it plainly, customers no longer think it's fair to give so much for so little in return.

The shift in consumer expectation is monumental, yet predictable. A meme has been floating around the internet over the last five years that perfectly encapsulates this trend. It's always captioned with a variation of "In hindsight, it wasn't worth giving Facebook all of my personal info to see pictures of my aunt's cat." Funny, yes. Insightful? Surprisingly so. Users want to receive something of equal value in return for their information.

That sense of fairness, specifically what the customer perceives as fair, is the driving force of this book. And it underscores why you can't just toss this issue over to legal and singularly focus on becoming compliant with regulations. Throughout this book, you'll begin to understand why that approach—as tempting as it may be—is nearsighted. These government regulations are the by-product of something much larger. And simply becoming compliant isn't enough to meet the expectations of your consumers.

The regulatory guardrails (and resulting requirements like increased user control of their own data) are all driven by what the consumer believes is and isn't fair. To win in a privacy-centric environment, marketers must have a keen understanding of how to create a fair value exchange.

Luckily, your buyers are more than happy to tell you what they want.

In 2021, the Boston Consulting Group (BCG) surveyed more than 1,000 consumers in the US and Canada and found that three things matter most to them.

1. *What* data is being collected
2. *Why* it is being collected
3. *How* the data is being collected[16]

16 Derek Rodenhausen et al., "Consumers Want Privacy. Marketers Can Deliver.," Boston Consulting Group, January 21, 2022, https://www.bcg.com/publications/2022/consumers-want-data-privacy-and-marketers-can-deliver.

These are reasonable concerns. How do you know whether the value proposition is fair if you don't know what you're being given in return? Consumers want to know what you know about them.

Transparency is a logical step in creating a fair-value proposition. Consumers want to know what their data is being used for. Will you be emailing them? Will you create a profile about them? Will you sell their information to someone else to do the same? Users want to understand how you're using their collected information.

We can think about the BCG survey results as the cover charge for our entry into the data acquisition club. It's the base level value you'll need to offer to receive data in return. And as you'll soon learn, whether that will be enough depends on your industry and how far into the future you want to propel your organization.

When we think of answering the questions above (what data is collected, why it is collected, and how it is collected), the clear first solution is greater transparency.

TRANSPARENCY

Imagine you walk into a supermarket to buy avocados. You pass through the doors, look right, and head to the produce aisle. As you pull an avocado off the shelf, you pause for a moment. Beneath the fruit is a black, circular lens. It's a camera (and obviously not for the purpose of store security).

Without you knowing, the store had been using your browsing data. For what purpose, you aren't entirely sure. You don't understand the need for secrecy. Why didn't they tell you about the camera? Did they intentionally hide it from you? It doesn't feel good to be secretly observed.

Curious and a little suspicious, you walk to a back room, open the door, and find an entire team watching various feeds from around the store.

Angry, you ask why the hell they are filming you.

To which they respond, "I'm not really sure, we were just told to record you." You've got to be kidding, right?

That's what happens when you implement a catch-all user data collection strategy with zero transparency. Remember the panelist in the last chapter who advised a marketer to collect as much information as they could and then figure out how to use it later? Cast a wide net, figure out what you're looking for, find it, and then likely sell the rest. While this strategy was effective for acquiring data, it didn't consider the customer.

Once you adopt the need for transparency, you tend to more closely examine what data you collect and why you are collecting it in the first place.

Imagine how you'd feel if things went a little differently. This time a grocer stopped you before you entered. They explained that to improve your buying experience, they would film you while in the store. When you asked why, they explained that by consenting to be on camera, you would receive a better selection of foods that interest you. Sounds like an improvement, right?

In the last chapter we told you that to make a fair value exchange, each party must understand what's asked of them. Your users can't make an informed decision without understanding why their data is being collected. You can't provide that information if you don't know what you're doing with it, either.

If you're going to be transparent by telling your users exactly how you're collecting data, you better also be ready to tell them what you're collecting and what it's being used for. You must be strategic and mindful about what information you actually want from your users and be ready to offer them something of equal value in return. Imagine if the store also informed you they were sending information about your height, age, and weight to diet supplement companies, who were then sending that data to your life insurance provider. You might be fine with the store using your information to provide you with better fruit options but may not be comfortable with them selling to a third party.

Transparency is the most fundamental component of a privacy-centric strategy. Consumers want organizations to be a window when it comes to their data, so that's what you should strive for.

The average person doesn't have a good understanding of things like cookies and network requests. So throwing a long-scrolling wall of text filled with jargon and legalese in the Terms of Agreement pop-up window isn't going to cut it (even if it does check some boxes when it comes to legal obligation—for now).

Real transparency means providing accessible information in plain language that informs the user. It means telling consumers what data is being collected, how it's used, who it's shared with, and what impact the collection of this data will have on them.

For example, if a person visits a company's website, a good

approach is a window that asks the user, "Are you just browsing, or would you like a personalized experience?" followed by a clear explanation of how collecting specific information such as product viewing and purchase history enables the company to deliver that experience. This level of transparency empowers the user to make an informed decision about whether that specific experience is worth sharing the requested information.

In the ideal end state, organizations are also strategic about *when* they request consumer data, only doing so when the information is relevant for both parties. For instance, maybe after the user in the previous example agrees to share the information needed for a personalized experience, they browse around. After they've viewed a few products, it's a good time for the site to then ask, "Would you like communications and reminders about the products you've browsed?" followed again by a brief explanation about how the company will use the information requested to do this.

When you're transparent with consumers, you build trust with them. Interactions like the examples described feel more like a dynamic conversation between your organization and consumers, enabling you to grow a relationship with each one and gain even more from future conversations. To maintain that relationship, it's not enough to simply tell consumers what you plan to do with their data. You have to give them a say too.

WHAT ABOUT THE FINE PRINT?

Sometimes our clients ask whether they can simply include the agreement to share consumer data with third parties in the "fine print" when someone accepts data collection on their site. The short answer is *it depends.* As of 2022, companies are required to disclose the sharing of data in some locations, like Europe, California, and Brazil, but not in others. But beyond any legal requirements, it's a best practice to be fully transparent with users beyond the fine print.

RESPECT USER CONTROL

Imagine if on entering the grocery store, someone presented you with multiple options. You could agree to have your data used to personalize the items offered to you, to receive offers on other foods you might like, or analyze your cart to see offers from other brands you might be interested in. Perhaps you check the first two boxes but decide to opt out of the third. This is user control.

Your approach to user control will undoubtedly be impacted by government regulations. For example, GDPR requires a user to give their explicit consent to the processing of their personal data, which includes collection. Meanwhile, other places with less stringent data protection laws (including some states within the US) do not guarantee the user the ability to opt out of collection but do give them control over how the data is used. As of 2022, there are still many countries without any data regulations whatsoever.

The directive that currently puts in place the most stringent guidance on collection is commonly called the EU cookie laws, referring to an EU directive requiring individual EU countries to create their own laws to cover provisions. The regulations put in place under the directive relate to disclosure and consent requirements in the accessing and use of cookies. So before any personal identifier is able to be assigned, stored, and collected, the user needs to make an explicit indication that they consent to the activity. Violations come with penalties, with

France fining Google and Meta $167 million and $69 million, respectively, for violating their ePrivacy law.[17]

At the time of writing, the US doesn't regulate consent as closely as the EU. Organizations can collect whatever they want, but in a few states a user has the right to opt out of specified activities, like selling their information and sharing for purposes of targeted advertising.

In Colorado, for example, a user has the right to opt out of any processing of their personal data for advertising based on their behavior across different websites, also known as targeted advertising. If we apply this to the in-store example used earlier, it means the store has the right to record the user's activity in the grocery store and personalize what's available to them on subsequent visits.

The user can't opt out of this personalization. But if the store is aggregating that information, or compiling information from various sources to create data sets to be processed, and then providing it to a partner that will use it for target advertising, the user can opt out.

It'd be like walking into that same grocery store and not being allowed to choose whether to be recorded but able to request that the grocery store not use their data to target them with weight loss supplements in another store, for example.

Based on the regulation and location of the user, they also have the right to request access to any information that has been

17 Jenny Colgate, "France Fines Facebook and Google for Violating the EU Cookie Law: You Need to Make It as Easy to Refuse as a Cookie, as It Is to Accept One," JD Supra, January 10, 2022, https://www.jdsupra.com/legalnews/france-fines-facebook-and-google-for-1858742/.

collected from them, as well as to request deletion of that information, which you may recall as "the right to be forgotten." In the case of an access request, it's important that your organization has the architecture in place to fulfill the request efficiently. In the case of a deletion request, it's critical that you can easily delete information without also deleting data that you aren't required to remove (we'll show you how in a later chapter). Access and deletion requests become very granular with respect to how information needs to be deleted, from whom, and who is responsible for doing so.

For now, understand that a percentage of your consumers likely have these rights. And if they don't currently, they will in the future. That means it's wise to begin setting up the architecture to complete these requests now. When a customer requests access, the data that you provide to them should be in a readable, usable format.

If you're requested to delete data, it's critical that it is deleted throughout the entire data supply chain (not just on your end). If you are currently sharing data with partners or selling to third parties, you must have the ability to delete it everywhere.

Consider how this might impact an e-commerce website. In this example, the site is using Google Analytics (GA) to understand how users interact with the site to improve user experience. This company then sends and stores the user data in Google BigQuery, a multi-cloud data warehouse, for later use by advertising platforms. If this organization receives a deletion request, they must delete from GA, BigQuery, and any additional advertising platforms that data has been shared with downstream.

Understanding how regulations will impact the data supply

chain is an important consideration for your organization. But what will this look like through the eyes of the consumer? Their experience comes down to user-centricity.

Historically, organizations have viewed consumer data with an ownership mindset. They tend to think that once the user has given information over, it belongs to the organization alone. This is not conducive to a privacy-centered strategy—and it's not true either.

Think of it like the difference between owning private land and using public land like a national forest. Generally, when you own private land, it belongs solely to you and is yours to do with as you will. When you visit a national forest, you are encouraged to be a steward of the land. You don't own it, you don't call the shots. But you also take care of it with a preservation mindset through practices like leave no trace. You also recognize these public spaces as valuable resources that need protection and respect.

When we talk about owning data, we mean "own" in a legal sense. But from a philosophical perspective, it's about stewardship. The information consumers provide you is their data, which means they expect to have the final say in what is collected, how it's used, and who has access to it. You're responsible for using that data to advance their experience.

To maintain trust with consumers, you also need to offer the ability to access and delete their personal information from your database. It's vital to make this process straightforward. Just as unclear terms in tiny print aren't transparent and don't earn you any favor from the consumer, neither does forcing them to jump through hoops to remove their data from your system—quite the opposite, actually.

To illustrate this, we conducted a little experiment. We don't take pride in calling out companies that aren't privacy-centered, so we won't name the businesses used for this exercise.

Soon after California passed its Consumer Privacy Act (CCPA), a friend who lives in California and an Ohio resident both decided to reach out to a number of retailers to access their personal data and then compare their experiences.

When the Ohio resident asked for their data, almost every retailer refused. Because of the consumer's location, these businesses were under no legal obligation to provide the information, so no harm, no foul.

The California resident had a different experience. California law requires retailers to provide a phone number for people who want access to their data. But when he called the number, all he got was a voice message that said, "Thank you for contacting us about your data. If you have a question, please leave a message and somebody will contact you."

When they eventually sent him the data he requested, the data wasn't even complete. The company only shared information about online visits, excluding any offline data about his in-store purchases. While this was compliant with the letter of the law, it didn't make for a good experience for someone who takes their privacy seriously.

Many companies are guilty of making it difficult for users to opt out of data collection or even to simply express their privacy preferences. That's in violation of many regulations and doing so can rub consumers the wrong way. Is having a person's data worth angering them to the point of boycotting your brand? We don't think so.

It's great to have a system in place to follow legal requirements, but why stop at the bare minimum? Rather than only doing what is necessary to avoid a lawsuit, a much more effective goal is to do what is necessary to be transparent and offer choices up front. Instead of only reacting to individual data access requests, now is the time to get proactive about anticipating those requests so you can optimize the experience of fulfilling them for both you and the consumers.

Of course, being a good steward of user data doesn't automatically mean users are going to hand their information over to you. You must incentivize consumers through value-add, and then deliver on it.

RESPECT IN YOUR ORGANIZATION

Respect is about adopting a transparent data collection strategy with your customer in mind. The issue is that even if respect is a core pillar of their business model, most organizations do not apply that principle to customer data. If your organization isn't prioritizing the elements of respect outlined in this chapter, it's a signal that you will be unprepared to compete in a privacy-centric future.

To win, respecting user data should be the foundation of any digital marketing strategy—not retroactively applied to clean up haphazard or non-compliant data collection.

When you respect user data, you make a clear declaration of what you're tracking and the key players in your organization understand why you're tracking it. You are aware of what data you'll use. Gone are the days of data collection without a plan.

Re-evaluate not only what you're tracking, but how you're using your data. Does your process respect your customers' expectation of privacy? On evaluation, you might even discover that the legally compliant practices you employ no longer fit into a culture of customer respect.

PRINCIPLE TWO: FIRST-PARTY OWNERSHIP OF FIRST-PARTY DATA

Imagine you own an airline. There are two passengers seated next to each other on a flight, and you spend the same number of advertising dollars to sell them their tickets. The first person purchased their ticket directly through your website, so you know a lot about them. You know whether the trip is for work or leisure. You know their birth date, credit card number, and their origin and destination. You even know how much they were willing to buy that ticket for. And now that you understand their preferences, you can market all kinds of other products to them.

But the person in the second seat is a different story. They purchased their ticket through a third-party vendor, which means you don't know anything about them at all. How are you supposed to market to them effectively without knowing the details of their trip? This underscores why first-party data is so critical. One of those passengers is going to potentially spend a lot of money with your brand, while the other might be just as expensive to market to and will be difficult to build a long-term relationship with.

Collecting first-party data isn't anything new. For a long time, organizations have understood the importance of information that comes directly from the consumer. We aren't proposing an overhaul, but rather shifting reliance on third-party data to first-party data.

In Chapter 5, we'll further explore the specifics of collecting, using, and truly owning your first-party data. The following section outlines fundamentals to consider as you build your data strategy.

USER-CENTRICITY AND RELATIONSHIPS

A friend of InfoTrust specializes in web design. Before she launches a new page, she puts it through the "grandma test" by asking whether her grandmother would be able to use the site confidently and efficiently. Could grandma navigate to the site, view a product, and ask a question? The grandma test ensures that every site our friend designs is user-centric.

Her test works for privacy design, too. If your grandparents are like many, they don't know much about cookies or trackers. A strong privacy-centric policy is one that all users understand. It's clear, accurate, and fair.

In practice, this means explaining that you collect information to personalize the shopping experience. It means telling the user that you collect information to provide recommendations based upon the products that they are viewing on the website. I want to collect information and assign an identifier so that I can remind you of products you liked from our website or provide you with offers as you navigate the rest of the internet.

At the heart of user-centricity is the ability to view privacy from the point of view of your consumer. It's not just about adhering to a regulation—it's about showing the user why the value exchange is mutually beneficial.

It can be just as important to tell the user what you *aren't* going to do with their data if they consent. Based on your organization's data policy, you might tell them that you will not sell their data to third parties.

Of course, if you tell your user you won't do something, you must make good on that promise. In the opening story of this chapter, you learned about a company that unknowingly broke their promise to the consumer. Even if it's accidental, a betrayal in trust can undermine the consumer-company relationship.

You don't have to break a promise to undermine your relationship. A massive text box of legalese can be as off-putting as a violation of trust. Keep your language direct, clear, and relevant.

In this traditional way of thinking, many organizations have taken a transactional approach with user data. The focus of data collection for performance advertising has been all about conversions, driving down cost per acquisition (CPA), and getting the best return on investment (ROI) for every dollar spent on marketing.

But data collection without the effort to understand your customers doesn't provide the best long-term ROI (or the best use of all that data you're working to collect). As consumers become more concerned with their privacy, they become increasingly selective about who they'll share their data with. If your transactions with a customer haven't done anything to build a relationship with them, why would they keep coming to you for future transactions, much less share their personal information with you?

To build a relationship, you must build trust. Being transparent and respecting user control are great starting points for this, but that alone won't keep a customer loyal to your brand.

In today's rapidly evolving landscape, the competitive advantage no longer goes to whoever can drive the most traffic for the lowest cost per acquisition. It now goes to who can earn more of the consumer's trust.

If Company A claims that transparency and trust are core pillars of its brand but only 5 percent of its user base opts to share data, while 20 percent of Company B's user base shares data, then it can be argued that Company B is doing a better job building relationships with customers. And with privacy now top of mind for consumers—and regulatory bodies enforcing rules around user-provided identifiers—Company A can't use technology to fill that 15 percent gap. There's no way to generate the same level of insights for customer preferences to best serve them.

Companies can't rely on a surveillance style of advertising anymore, so you have to build your understanding of your customers through direct interactions with them. The best way to do that? Communication.

USER DATA PROTECTION

Pretend you and a friend just walked into a gym that you're both interested in joining. You check out the equipment and soon, a salesperson comes over. After discussing the class offerings and operating hours, you talk about price.

The salesperson turns to you and says, "Your monthly membership fee will be fifty euros."

He then turns to your friend and says, "Yours is sixty euros."

Perplexed, you ask why. He tells you that rates are based on diet. You look at each other quizzically, until you remember your last trip to the supermarket. You bought pizza and beer, while your friend purchased organic avocados and chicken. Based on this data, the gym is making an assumption that your friend is willing to spend more money on health-related activities and products.

How does the gym know this, though? You return to the supermarket and ask whether they sold your data. The store assures you that they did not and reviews their privacy policy with you. You realize that this gym must have somehow dubiously acquired your purchase history from the grocery store.

This might sound dystopian, but something similar happened in real life. In 2020, Meta sued BrandTotal and Unimania for data scraping user accounts.[18] The AI used by these companies also targeted other social media companies, including Twitter, Amazon, LinkedIn, and YouTube.

Scraping is the act of analyzing public data from websites using AI. Any time you enter a query into a search engine, AI performs a scrape of all websites with matching keywords. This technique extends beyond search engines. Want a bunch of information about housing costs in your area? Scrape Zillow.

18 Jessica Romero, "Taking Legal Action Against Data Scraping," Meta, October 1, 2020, https://about.fb.com/news/2020/10/taking-legal-action-against-data-scraping/.

Want to know more about your favorite sports teams? Scrape ESPN. (It is important to note that not all scraping should be considered ethical and/or legal—it all depends upon the usage of the data gained and the terms of service for the entity from which data is being scraped.)

A car insurance company using a questionable data policy can technically buy scraped data about your consumers from third-party platforms. Based on their photos, you can even assess risk. Is there often alcohol in their hand? Are most of their photos taken at night? Do they like fast cars and motorcycles? If so, this person is then put into a higher risk category and quoted a higher price on insurance. All of this happens without their knowledge or consent.

In the last chapter, we suggested that because data used to be cheap and ubiquitous, we didn't always care for it properly. This is in part why, historically, data protection protocols haven't been put in place in many industries.

Today it's impossible to complete a transaction without sharing personal data. Your name, address, and credit card information accompany nearly every online purchase. Threats like phishing, social engineering attacks, and password and identity theft all highlight the importance of having the appropriate data privacy strategy to ensure the protection of customers' personal information is guaranteed.

There are so many reasons to ensure proper protection. From significant fines to destroyed credibility, failing to guard user data is a serious concern. Many of the largest GDPR fines issued to date are related to insufficient protections for user data and resulting breaches. In 2020 British Airways was fined 20 million British pounds for their failure to prevent a massive data breach that exposed the personal data of 400,000 employees and customers.[19]

But a lack of protection also impacts the relationship you have with your customers. If users believe their privacy is at risk, they will be reluctant to share the information you need to better serve them. Clear rules about how data is collected, stored, protected, and managed—as well as enforcement of those rules—will make it easier for consumers to trust brands, especially as we move forward in an age where brand trust will be increasingly important.

With the expectation of data privacy and security becoming the new normal, and as personal information becomes more difficult to obtain, it's worth asking the question:

Do we really need to collect all this data in the first place?

USER DATA MINIMIZATION

You're back at the supermarket. But this time, someone comes up behind you and slaps a Post-It note on your back that reads "Customer X14e9". As you walk through the produce aisle, you pick up an orange, decide you don't want it, and continue to the checkout. Once there, the clerk says, "You forgot the oranges! Would you like to purchase them now?"

This is the fundamental premise of an online identifier.

The principle of data minimization asks whether there is another

19 Joe Tidy, "British Airways Fined £20M over Data Breach," *BBC*, published October 16, 2020, https://www.bbc.com/news/technology-54568784.

way to gain the same insight without identifiers. Is there a better way to uncover similar information? In data minimization, organizations figure out the minimum amount of information needed to gain the insights they need to market effectively.

There is no debating that leaving third-party cookies behind in your digital marketing strategy will reduce the volume of data you collect. While this means you'll have to adopt new strategies, a reduced volume doesn't have to be a bad thing. Third-party data was already the least personal and least accurate data in your marketing toolkit.

A strong privacy strategy will also increase the value of data you collect. New technologies offer marketers tools that can give them the same outcome while still being compliant with government regulations and consumer expectations. For example, instead of using trackers to target based on specific past behaviors across the internet, marketers can instead target based on a general inference about interests. Or they can optimize for the campaign instead of the individual.

PRINCIPLE THREE: ACTION BASED ON INSIGHT AND UNDERSTANDING

Conversations are key to building lasting relationships, whether it's between people, organizations, or both. Obviously it's not realistic for every organization to hire people to individually speak with every customer, but luckily that's not necessary. What *is* necessary is improving your data collection methods to more closely resemble an organic conversation.

The conventional methods for collecting data are more like an interrogation than a conversation. Imagine two people talking, but one of them only asks questions like, "Name? Date of birth? Location? Health status?" Requesting all this information at once without any real-time consideration for the answers creates a very one-sided interaction—one that many people don't want to have with a stranger or a bot. That's what leads consumers to enter false information associated with fake email accounts in web forms.

But what if you were able to show users that you care about their answers?

For example, imagine if the grocery store's website offered a quiz that shoppers can take if they want ingredient recommendations. It could start with a question like "What do you like to cook?" and provide options for users to select, like comfort food, seafood, Italian, Mexican, and health food. Then, based on the selected answer, the next questions could ask about any allergies.

All of this is personal data, but now the user can clearly see the benefit of sharing accurate information because of the two-sided nature of the interaction. This enables you to deliver a superior experience to the user, keeping the conversation going and growing your relationship with them.

This shift in your data collection methodology is essentially a shift from short-term value creation to long-term value creation. Rather than working to get as many clicks as possible so that you can use tracked data for remarketing that generates sales, now you're working with more relevant, targeted information collected in a way that feels more natural to the consumer and builds trust with them. This method gives you information that you can work with more deeply on a regular basis moving forward.

We know this quality-over-quantity method works because we've experienced it on both the business side and on the consumer side.

When one of the authors was shopping to lease a car, he visited a couple of dealerships to compare offers. The first dealership utilized the traditional interrogation-style method of collecting information. The salesperson asked him about his budget, the features he was looking for, and whether he was interested in any particular features before showing him brochures for specific cars.

The second dealership's salesperson was much more effective and made a lasting impression (so much so that he still remembers the salesperson's name years later). He even distinctly remembers him saying, "Come on over, let's have a conversation. Tell me what your day looks like." The salesperson explained that he wanted to understand his driving habits and routines. He asked questions like whether he enjoyed driving to other cities, the furthest he would be willing to drive for a vacation, and other lifestyle questions related to car usage. Of course he was trying to make a sale, but it felt like more than that. He genuinely wanted to help pick the best car for the author's needs. He cared about the experience.

As the conversation wrapped up he said, "Obviously, you can choose whatever car you want, but I would recommend a hybrid since you don't really drive that much. You don't need a lot of miles per year. Since you don't have bikes or other big sports gear to load, we should look at models for urban driving rather than an outdoorsy car. And you don't have pets or kids, so if you're looking for something nicer, we can look at cars that focus on interior comfort." He gathered so much information about the author's daily life that he could recommend a car that suited him very well.

Years later, when the author was ready for a new car, he texted that same salesperson. One of the first questions he asked was, "Has anything changed in your life?" He asked about marriage and kids—not to pry, but to assess how well the current car met his needs and how they had changed since they last spoke. That's what a relationship-centered experience built on conversations looks like, and it won him a loyal client who trusts him and recommends him to others.

How many other customers are loyal to that salesperson because of the experience he consistently provides? We'd wager: a lot. That's the value of quality over quantity when it comes to using consumer data. What good does sending your marketing emails to fake email accounts do? Wouldn't you rather invest your time and resources into replicating conversational experiences that have customers enthusiastically sharing their interests and preferences with you? The long-term ROI is greater than the short-term ROI of rapid data collection—plus, you don't have to worry about whether you're in compliance when the customer is happy to share details about themselves with you.

Of course, that means you must maintain a relationship with your customers. Relationship-centered data collection methods are not a one-and-done deal. But that's a good thing, because it means the experience becomes more valuable for you both over time.

For example, consider what it's like trying to get a nice gift for a good friend compared to selecting a gift for someone you barely know. It's much easier to get the reaction you want to the gift when you know the person well, right? You only get to know a person that well by interacting with them repeatedly and on a deeper level. It's the same with customers.

Great examples of businesses implementing this strategy well include clothing companies like Trunk Club and Stitch Fix. The core value proposition of these brands is the relationship between the customer and the company stylists assigned to them. The more they work together to shop for clothes, the better the stylist's understanding of the customer's preferences becomes, enabling them to select clothes that the customer is more likely to purchase in future transactions.

Of course, no matter how great your first-party data acquisition strategy is, you won't always have all the data you want. That's why you'll learn how to model to fill the gaps in a later chapter.

Implementing a privacy-centered strategy that prioritizes user experience takes time. We're not suggesting you redesign your entire brand's website and marketing materials overnight, but you do owe it to your brand to start thinking about how to create these relationships. What kind of questions can you ask your customers to help them make more informed purchase decisions that they're more likely to be happy with?

PRACTICE SELF-IMPROVEMENT

Privacy is becoming a cornerstone of the consumer experience. We hope by this point we've demonstrated why striving for compliance alone is insufficient when it comes to adapting your marketing strategy. Improving your privacy experience is something you should consistently strive for. Now is the time to start experimenting.

At the end of the day, the most successful marketing companies are the ones that experiment more often. A/B testing is an important strategy, but it's crucial not to focus only on comparing benchmarks. You want to create an ongoing culture of experimentation where you find ways to test multiple new ideas for the sake of learning new information and always self-improving, not just improving a single aspect of your operations in a single instance.

Maybe your clothing brand can't afford to hire stylists for every single customer right now, but can you schedule some Zoom consultations for a sampling of your customers? Perhaps instead of having customers fill out a form immediately upon visiting your website, you can create quizzes for the different needs your products serve and let them know about it.

These are just a couple examples to illustrate small-scale changes you can make to test the waters. The sooner you experiment, the sooner you have the information you need to properly adapt. Chaos is a ladder, so now is the perfect time to give any and every idea a chance. The information gathered from experiments like these may surprise you, and that insight will be vital to building a privacy-centered strategy that helps you win over your customers and ultimately sell more products and services.

PREPARE FOR TOMORROW

One thing is certain about the future: regulations will change, new technologies will be invented, and data acquisition will remain a core part of enabling marketing strategy. But the way in which we acquire that data is going to change. That inevitable transformation should be built on strong, privacy-centric principles that respect customer data.

So what does it really mean for an organization to value user privacy? And how do these differ from standard principles like respect and transparency?

InfoTrust's privacy principles are not generic or obscure. For example, "respect the consumer" could have various interpretations outside of privacy, like providing quality products or great customer service. The problem is that it's too broad to address your customers' privacy concerns. That's why you need a foundation that incorporates privacy-specific language.

Baked into these foundations is a demand for better data practices. And once you bake that necessary transformation into the architecture of your organization, you only need to reference these three principles to decide whether a new targeting strategy or shift in policy is acceptable to you.

In May of 2018, we witnessed a data privacy breach throw a wrench into a large, global company based in the EU. This was around the time GDPR was beginning to take full effect in Europe. During a meeting discussing how to transition a global company's current data strategy into compliance with the new GDPR guidelines, a very flustered employee walked in with a paper in his hands.

The executive's face fell as she reviewed the printed PDF. For the next two days, management instructed every employee to stop what they were doing and triage. They briefed customer service and gave them talking points, told marketing to assess reputational damage, and looked to data strategists to create a fast solution. It was chaos.

So what was this document that caused such turmoil?

A user had installed a browser extension that allowed them to identify any trackers on a website (there are many free plugins downloadable online) and then navigated to the client's site. Once on the landing page, the user activated the plugin and watched a list of about fifteen different data trackers pop up.

The user then opted out of trackers across the site. This is where the story gets messy. When the user again activated the extension to see whether the site complied, they were surprised to find the trackers were still enabled. Tracking after opting out is in direct violation of EU guidelines, and the PDF was proof of a violation. But there was something even bigger stirring beneath this story.

If you walked into that organization after the document circulated, you would have thought someone pulled the fire alarm. Everyone was on high alert, certain they should be doing something (what exactly that something was, wasn't clear).

The marketing team was especially distraught. No one understood the potential repercussions. If word got out, could the brand ever recover? Were they about to be fired? Few team members in analytics even understood how trackers work, which platforms were running, or what data was being collected, let alone how to fix it.

At the time, the organization was just implementing the same tactics as everyone else: they employed third-party cookies and trackers to collect user data. They were still nascent in the overall privacy-centric strategy journey and were heavily reliant on third-party technology, as well as traditional methods of activation and measurement.

Unfortunately, many of these activities weren't compliant with government regulations.

If they'd had a privacy-centric data strategy in place, they would never have gotten into this situation. In fact, if they had enacted just one of our three privacy principles, they would have realized that they needed to revisit their value exchange.

SUMMARY OF PRINCIPLES

Principle One: Respect the Rights of Users

Users have a baseline set of privacy rights as defined in laws and regulations. At minimum you must respect these. Success in the privacy-centric reality is predicated on a mutual trust relationship with your consumers—there is no mutual trust without mutual respect. Privacy-centric data strategy accomplishes business use cases while meeting the privacy expectations of your consumers.

Principle Two: First-Party Ownership of First-Party Data

First-party data is critical to execute in the privacy-centric world. The collection of this data requires a strong relationship with consumers and a compelling value exchange so they will consent and provide valuable preference information. Once collected you must protect user data with the utmost care and own the end-to-end system within which data flows.

Principle Three: Action Based on Insight and Understanding

The deprecation of persistent third-party identifiers means reliance on technology to track and target in a one-to-one context is largely outdated. Effective organizations must have an intimate understanding of their consumers. Mining insights from compliantly collected first-party data is the means of getting to a deeper understanding. These insights are what all marketing and advertising decisions must be based on.

CHAPTER THREE

TRANSFORM YOUR ORGANIZATION TO MEET THE NEW REALITIES

CHAPTER CONTRIBUTOR: CHRIS VAUGHAN

Chris Vaughan is the Director of Strategy at InfoTrust, working with his team to develop rock-solid strategic plans that ensure the company remains the leader in privacy-centric analytics solutions.

Prior to this role, Chris served as InfoTrust's Head of Vertical for CPG, FMCG, and Multi-brand partners, where he helped the world's largest and most recognizable brands develop, deploy, and measure their digital analytics strategies. Throughout his career, Chris has influenced the digital analytics architectures, data collection methodologies, and insights for thousands of websites and mobile apps around the world.

As a husband and father of three girls, Chris enjoys spending time with his family, working out, and traveling (especially to the Caribbean).

CHAPTER CONTRIBUTOR: PETER CROFUT

Peter Crofut is the Director of Partnerships at InfoTrust overseeing the company's partnership with Google. As Google's former Chief Platforms Evangelist, he partnered with the C-Suite of Google's largest brands to accelerate their digital display, data, and analytics transformations.

Peter is recognized as a pioneer and expert in the intersection of data analytics, cloud, and display platform technologies. His thought leadership has been published in *Forbes* and Think with Google; he also guest lectures at some of the world's top business schools and industry forums.

During a presentation about a consent mode implementation project, a client asked us, "Are we supposed to become a privacy company now? We're a consumer–packaged goods business, not a tech company. We're not really built for all this."

This mindset was the main reason behind continuous delays in the project. With a business concerned primarily with manufacturing and selling products, there is no clear answer to where in the organization data privacy should be handled. Is this within the legal team's scope or should it belong to marketing? Who should be running it? How fundamental should data privacy be to my overall business strategy?

Researchers attempted to answer this question. They analyzed how financial markets evaluate firms' data privacy strategies. Based on their insights, they created an inverted U-shaped graph, with the left side representing too little privacy, the right too much privacy, and the middle as the optimal data strategy for every organization. They claimed that the ideal practice was to do no more or no less than the competition. The authors argued that this would ensure that organizations met the bare minimum while keeping costs low.[20]

Perhaps looking at your neighbor's lawn to decide whether to water or fertilize the grass more or less is a good enough strategy for lawn care. But for something as important as data privacy, organizations need a better way to craft a strategy that is customized to their specific needs.

Ultimately, it's your organization's decision on how central a role privacy will play. There is a spectrum. Some businesses will choose to do what is required and compete in other areas. Others will turn privacy into a competitive advantage. To figure out where privacy fits into your organization, use the strategic choice cascade.

20 Pavlos A. Vlachos, Panagiotis Avramidis, and Nikolaos G. Panagopoulos, "How to Optimize Your Company's Approach to Data Privacy," *Harvard Business Review*, August 26, 2020, https://hbr.org/2020/08/how-to-optimize-your-companys-approach-to-data-privacy.

STRATEGIC CHOICE CASCADE

When discussing overall business strategy, we use five questions that we call the strategic choice cascade. (This model was outlined in Playing to Win by A.G. Lafley.[21])

Strategic Choice Cascade

1. What is our winning aspiration?
2. Where will we play?
3. How will we win?
4. What capabilities must we have?
5. What management systems do we need?

We present these questions as a cascade because each is an aspect of the one above it, all the way to the top. This is important when thinking about where to position privacy in your overall business strategy.

The first question refers to the company's market position. A winning aspiration is the ultimate goal of the organization. All subsequent elements of the strategy are meant to support accomplishing the winning aspiration. This is one place a company can choose to put privacy. If you want to place "protecting your users' data" as your primary selling point, then privacy is a winning aspiration.

But chances are that much like our clients, your organization already has a winning aspiration. It's probably to be the best at providing a particular good or service, with a specific method for how to do that. In that case, we argue that privacy needs to

---

21 Roger L. Martin, "Strategic Choices Need to Be Made Simultaneously, Not Sequentially," *Harvard Business Review*, April 3, 2017, https://hbr.org/2017/04/strategic-choices-need-to-be-made-simultaneously-not-sequentially.

become a core value of your company to support your winning aspiration. Let's consider what that looks like with the rest of the cascade.

The second question addresses your market directly. If you're doing business in a specific region, you need to know the privacy laws of that market. This is true even if you're in multiple markets or regions. So, privacy *does* impact this part of your overall strategy, but it determines how much you need to know (not how you manage data privacy).

The last three questions are the most complex because they refer to the methods for accomplishing your winning aspiration. If privacy is not your winning aspiration (but likely is still part of how you will win and your organization's strategic capabilities), this is where it will come into play in your overall strategy. You'll have a lot to consider:

- How can you turn privacy and analytics into a competitive edge to win in your market?
- How important do you want this to be to your relationship with consumers?
- Who in your organization should be involved in working with your customers' data?
- How much of the data infrastructure are you capable of building yourself?

We know it's a lot to think about, especially if data privacy has never been a significant consideration for you before. That's why we've put together a framework with some example cases to help you consider privacy's place in your overall strategy.

THE 6 "P"S OF DIGITAL ANALYTICS TRANSFORMATION

We call The 6 "P"s a transformation framework because regardless of where privacy falls on your strategic choice cascade, you need to transform your marketing strategy to be privacy-compliant. If privacy is not already a capability your company has, now is the time to develop it. And if you do already have some structure in place, our handy alliteration will help you evaluate its effectiveness.

The 6 "P"s include purpose, people, platforms, process, pace, and payoff.

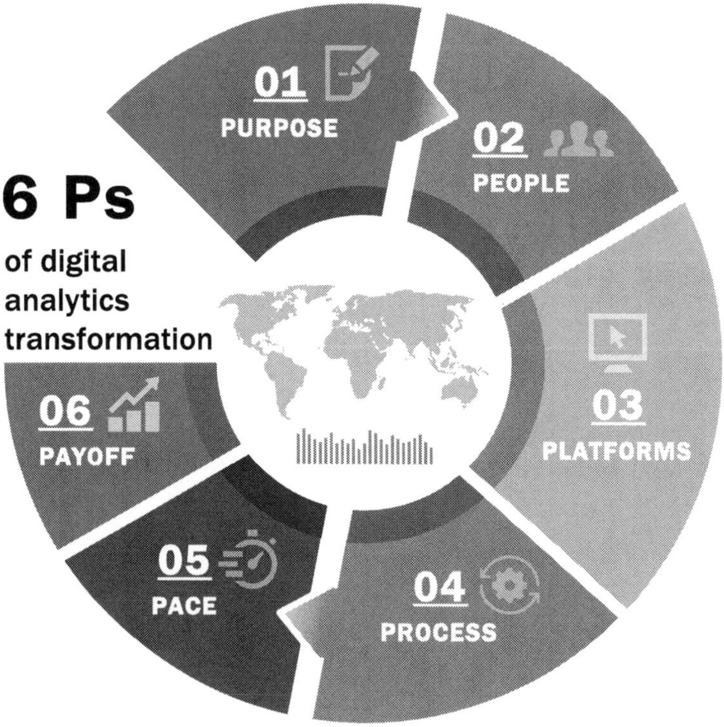

© InfoTrust

Use The 6 "P"s to help understand what components your data strategy needs to include. We'll cover each together, beginning with purpose.

PURPOSE

Why are you building a privacy strategy?

Perhaps it's to become compliant. Or maybe you personally value privacy and want to reflect that in your marketing. Or you could intend to use it as a selling point for building better relationships with your customers. It could even be all of the above.

Your purpose is the context framing the steps you take for building your strategy. Make sure you're clear on exactly what it is you want before you move on to the next step.

A good place to start with this is your winning aspiration. For example, we have a client launching new connected devices in the beauty industry. The market for this kind of thing isn't very big (at least, not at the time of this writing), so this company's winning aspiration is to create more connected devices in the beauty space and to become the top provider of that when the market grows.

The target audience for these products is people who take their love of self-care and beauty to the next level. Innovative technology like what this client is creating isn't cheap, so the community of people who purchase these devices will have a sense of exclusivity about it. This allows the company to invest in building close relationships with each of its customers, earning their brand loyalty and trust.

Part of the brand's strategy to achieve this is to protect user data collected through its devices—and use that as a big selling point for its products. The purpose of creating a privacy-centered data strategy is to support those ongoing relationships the company wants to build with consumers. See how it's all connected?

The "why" is important because when it's missing, this aspect is always going to be somebody else's problem. That's how you get delays caused by lack of ownership like the consent mode implementation project we mentioned at the start of the chapter.

PEOPLE

If you don't know and can't quickly find the answers to all of these questions for your organization, there's room for improvement in your digital analytics strategy.

Many clients we've worked with have wanted to start their strategy improvements by looking at tools (platforms) and methods (processes), but this is a common pitfall.

People is the first P after purpose because you really need to start with people. Following are a few questions to help you evaluate who should be responsible for your privacy strategy.

- Who oversees your organization's consumer data?
- Do you know who to go to for access requests?
- Who handles policy and regulation updates?
- Is all that data managed in-house or do you work with a partner organization?
- If it's the latter, do you know who you should talk to about your data?

If you don't establish a solid multifunctional team to take ownership of using your company's consumer data to support your purpose, no amount of tools or processes will make you more effective. Starting with data governance council formation is critical to successfully transforming your digital analytics strategy.

This is especially true for large enterprises. One of our clients is a conglomerate with several companies that each have consumer-facing websites. This company's goal is to have first-party ownership of all data coming in through its various websites to comply with regulations and better preserve the trust of its customers.

Getting the Right Teams Involved

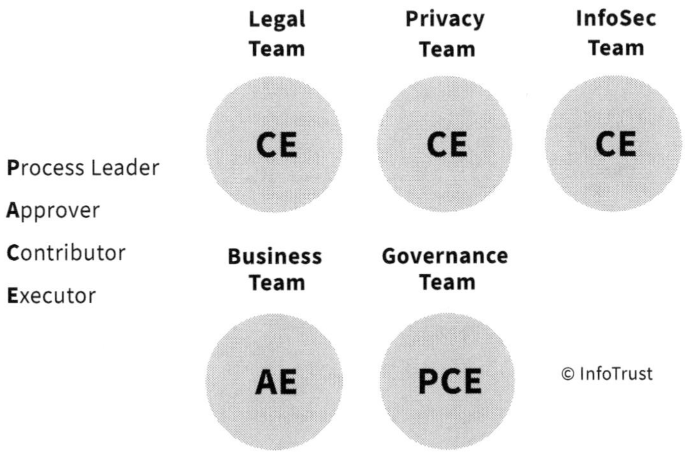

Creating and fully owning the data pipeline from the point of collection all the way through the point of value realization and activation is a massive undertaking for an operation of this size, so it's vital to start by creating an organized and qualified governance team to accomplish this.

As we've already hinted at in this chapter, there are multiple places through which data flows in your organization, which means there need to be multiple people on your data governance team. You'll want to make sure this includes a legal expert who can stay on top of compliance with privacy regulations, an IT expert to oversee the infrastructure of the analytics architecture, and a marketing person who knows how to analyze that data to generate insights that your brand can use effectively—to name just a few. We haven't even mentioned the business owners or other roles because while the roles we've shared are the most common foundation, this team and its hierarchy looks different for every enterprise.

Consider what you want to outsource. Building the capability to manage data at every stage of the data flow process is not easy, and it's not always practical for a business to do it completely in-house. For some companies it makes sense to have only an internal team for data governance, while others are better off working with partner organizations in a multi-partner orchestration. When that happens, it's important to find the right partner—usually more than one because often one company is not equipped to do everything well at both the activation and enablement stages (more on that in the data flow section later).

To determine your company's unique needs for the data governance council, start by figuring out who is in charge. Who is the person responsible for signing off on all the decisions about your privacy implementation? Ownership is the biggest holdup in projects like this, so it's important to address this first.

Once you've settled that, you're ready to identify who else needs to be part of the data governance council. To begin, map the current flow of consumer data through your organization. We refer to the flow of consumer data as an analytics value chain. This chain has three main stages: acquisition, enablement, and activation.

Acquisition refers to raw data collection, such as when a consumer enters their information in a form on your website. Enablement refers to the process of interpreting data to generate insights from it. Activation refers to how those insights are used. In marketing, this includes actions like running email campaigns, executing display advertising, and any other paid media efforts.

We find that it's most effective to map your digital analytics value chain in reverse order, so let's start with activation.

Activation

Who is going to be using the outputs from analytics? How will these outputs be used to accomplish your organization's purpose? For example, if you want to leverage insights to make marketing decisions, then the person responsible for activation is probably the leader of your marketing team. So they should be on your council, too.

Enablement

Who is responsible for generating the insights the activation person is using? What platforms are being used? Oftentimes the responsibility for generating insights sits with a data science or business analysis team, while architecture sits with engineering or IT.

Acquisition

Going back further in the chain, who is responsible for getting the data to the enablement people? This is usually the people at the front end responsible for collecting the data, typically an implementation partner like InfoTrust. Whether this person is internal or external, they should also be working with your data governance council.

There are other considerations in the data flow as well, such as taking regulatory requirements into consideration. Whether they're internal or external, you should have someone who can provide expertise about what you're legally allowed to collect, how you can collect it, how you're allowed to use it, and so on. This expert and the person who makes decisions based on this expertise (if they're not the same person) should also be working with your council.

In short, any decision maker responsible for data as it flows through your organization (and partners) should be involved.

It's not uncommon for clients to do this analytics value chain mapping exercise and realize they don't actually know where all of the touchpoints are for data flowing in their organization. If you don't know, then your first task is to find out.

We often suggest multi-partner orchestration to accomplish your outcomes, especially for enablement and activation. Companies that are good at interpreting data to generate insights at the enablement stage are not always well equipped to help you act on those insights, and vice versa. These stages require a very different skill set, so while it's not impossible to find one company that can do it all, it's often better to find one that specializes and has a good understanding of your industry, market, and technology used at the respective stages of the analytics value chain. Just be sure that none of the organizations you partner with sell the data they work with—otherwise you can't really guarantee privacy for your consumers.

Whether you plan to include partners or not, it's important to also ensure that the people on your data governance council are properly trained. We've already discussed how the data privacy environment is drastically changing at a breakneck pace. That means a team that is knowledgeable right now won't stay that way if you don't account for the need to upskill as things change. Make sure you know who on your team is responsible for keeping everyone briefed so that you can institutionalize knowledge on data privacy and not solely rely on a partner or individual.

PLATFORMS

Once you've identified who should be working on your council, you're ready to move on to the tools (platforms) phase of your digital analytics transformation. Consider your current infrastructure for data flow. Do you have the full stack you need to effectively identify your most valuable users and target them? If not, should you build one or buy existing products? (Spoiler: probably the latter, but this is also unique to your organization.)

Similar to people, your platform setup is also best evaluated through mapping the analytics value chain in your organization. This time, instead of focusing on who interacts with the data in the acquisition, enablement, and activation stages, you want to focus on what platforms are used for collection, distribution, analysis, and integration of the data within those stages (in the forward order this time).

To start with acquisition, you want to make sure to use a consent management platform (like OneTrust, Usercentrics, or TrustArc) at the point of collection to ensure data is collected according to the user's privacy preferences—and that the collection and usage of the data is transparent with the user (see Chapter 5 for what that entails). Then the data will flow through a data distribution platform (like Rudderstack™ or Google Tag Manager) to your first-party data warehouse, as well as any third-party platforms you're working with. The first-party data warehouse and third-party platforms will be the platforms in which interaction and user data across different digital touchpoints are aggregated and analyzed.

As you enter the enablement stage, you're likely distributing some of that collected data to a consumer data platform, which is a tool to aggregate all of the consumer data you have from your digital properties into one place in the format that you need. Then you can move on to platforms to help you do the more advanced data enrichment and analysis to generate those important insights based on user information.

The truth is, you're probably not currently well equipped to accomplish all of this in a privacy-centric way. You picked up this book for a reason, right? The current standard of data practices at the time of this writing just aren't built for that, so your current architecture is likely inadequate. Therefore, in the process of mapping how data flows through your organization, you'll need to perform a gap analysis to figure out what needs to change.

Some questions to ask for this gap analysis include:

- Does the platform have the capability to enable you to reach your stated end goal?

- Is it accomplishing what it needs to without outsourcing ownership?
- Does it allow you to respect user control?
- Does it align with your compliance needs?

Once you've identified the gaps, the question becomes whether you should build or buy the solution. Keep in mind that you shouldn't just consider cost when deciding this. Building a solution is costly up front and can be more costly over time if it's not easy to modify as developments in practices and regulations occur.

Let's look at another example to illustrate what this looks like. (For this example, we'll use the names of some of the current market leaders at the time of this writing, but you might have different platform options to consider depending on when you're reading this.)

Consider a car company with multiple dealerships that wants to optimize its data pipeline for privacy. To acquire the full set of tools needed, the company should start by considering consent management platforms (CMPs) that can help manage user choice and disclosure for compliant data collection. A CMP like OneTrust can help to do this in a way that makes it easier to adjust disclosures and consent experiences as requirements change across markets.

Once the consumer can make an informed choice regarding their data sharing preferences, a company can then make the decision of what platforms to use to facilitate the end-to-end process of extracting value from the data available. If the decision is made to buy the tech stack in full, there are a number of solutions to consider.

For data collection and distribution, the company may use a server-side tag management system like server-side Google Tag Manager or RudderStack. These systems can send data directly to an analytics platform like Google Analytics 4, an activation platform like Google Ads, *and* an owned first-party marketing data warehouse built in Google Cloud with Google BigQuery.

Once in the company-owned cloud environment, data science teams can leverage Google Cloud solutions like Vertex AI to generate insights to inform marketing decisions, while analytics teams can leverage visualization tools such as Looker to report on user behavior and media campaign effectiveness.

Data Flow

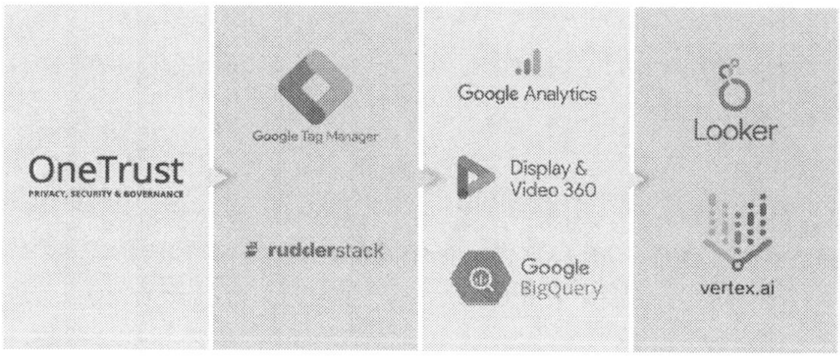

© InfoTrust

This part you're probably more familiar with: once the car company has gathered the insights to inform its next campaign, it's ready to start marketing on the media platforms its target consumers are using, like Google, Facebook, and YouTube.

When building out your stack, make sure you don't spend too much time overanalyzing your different platform options. The time to build your privacy-centric strategy is now, so don't get held up comparing minute details between vendors when most of your options are going to check all the same boxes. If you're worried about monitoring the quality of your data and ensuring that everything is working the way it should, then you can go with something like Tag Inspector to help with the creation and monitoring of the data map.

PROCESS

If a customer anywhere in the world requests access to the data your company has on them, how long would it take you to fulfill that request? What processes are in place for you to comply? Do you know all the steps necessary to do it correctly and efficiently?

By this point, you've established your purpose, outlined a data map, identified the key players who need to be involved with your data governance council, and selected the platforms that will help you accomplish your goals. Now it's time to form the processes you need to extract value and ensure that your privacy-centric core principles are being met efficiently. Processes are what hold together the ecosystem of people and platforms you've created. This part of the framework is about focusing on the delivery.

- How do you get the data from Point A to Point B to Point C and so on?
- How do you determine the access rights of the people on the data governance council?
- How do you stay on top of the access rights of the users?
- Who can do what with your consumers' data?
- How do you modify this process for users who only partially opt in to the things you want to use their data for?

- How do you manage users who previously opted in but now want to opt out?
- How do you document changes in privacy requirements and notify your users?

All of these questions reveal processes you need to have in place to handle situations that come up with collecting and using consumer data.

It's important to have technical and operational safeguards in place to make sure that your data is always complete, accurate, and compliant.

There is a difference between *becoming* compliant and *staying* compliant. You can get compliant only to be pushed out of compliance by new legal changes or updates. This can easily happen if you don't know how to properly respond and modify accordingly. With the rapid pace of change in the current landscape, compliance isn't easy to maintain on your own if you're not an expert.

This is the main reason custom-built internal infrastructure can quickly become antiquated. It's not typically made to be a durable infrastructure in which you can plug new solutions into the ecosystem.

This problem is more common than you might expect. We once met with a luxury jewelry retailer that had been using the same point-of-sale system for two decades. The reason? Nobody on the current staff knew how to modify the website, so updating it would require rebuilding the entire thing from scratch.

This isn't sustainable in a privacy-centric world. If a user requests access to their data, you need to know exactly how to find every bit of information you have on them and export it to them. And if they want you to delete their data, you need to make sure you know how to get it out of every part of your ecosystem. If you don't, you're going to have a problem.

We know this can be kind of overwhelming to think about, so we put together a matrix to help you visualize what you should be thinking about in the processes part of the framework.

PROCESS	COLLECTION	DISTRIBUTION	ENRICHMENT	ACTIVATION
Access Request	What data was collected from the user?	Where (platforms) did that data go?	How was the data used?	What outcomes resulted from using the user's data? Where else did you send any insights or their data?

PACE

If a new regulation on data privacy passed today, how quickly could you adapt?

Adaptability is critical to staying compliant in the current environment. If you can't quickly make changes, what's holding you up? How can you change that?

This part of the framework is where the importance of experimentation comes in.

- How fast are you able to test new ideas, products, and solutions?
- How often are you able to conduct new experiments?

- Is there anything from the previous Ps holding up new pilots?

If so, your ecosystem isn't efficient and you're not moving fast enough. You want to get to a point of rapid experimentation and rapid adaptability to the changing technical and regulatory landscape. This is how your team will drive change and stand out from the competition.

A good example of the importance of pace is the ability to activate data based on different audiences. It's no secret that segmentation is key to successful marketing; you want to get the right ad to the right person. What defines the right person? Those who fall into a certain segment based on demographics, preferences, and whatever other factors that are relevant to your company.

The possibilities for those factors—and their level of relevancy—are huge. If you want to experiment with using those different attributes to inform your marketing decisions, you can't spend too much time on analysis and ownership. You need to be able to quickly create new segments, conduct experiments, collect the results, and adjust accordingly. If you're too slow, you could negatively impact the business's bottom line.

PAYOFF

How can you better serve your customers with the digital tools available online?

We hope that by now it's clear that the payoff for investing in a privacy-centric strategy goes well beyond not getting sued. Compliance is important, but this transformation will also impact your bottom line, your ROI on resources, your customers' experience, and your operational excellence. New digital business models may result in new revenue sources. Transparency and improved customer relationships should translate into more revenue. You should be able to better perform certain tasks more efficiently.

In the long term, protecting user privacy gives you a competitive advantage that can ultimately help you win over a larger consumer base.

The key to reaping all these benefits is to make sure that your payoff is tied to your purpose, not just your bottom line. You have to go back to that "why" you formed at the start of this framework. It informs what you need to be measuring. If you do not have a clear definition of success, you won't know when you've reached it.

Now is the time to measure your current capabilities and make a plan for long-term success. Start building your data governance team. Companies succeed by having the right people, not by having the most tools. Perform a gap analysis, then build a scalable and uncluttered platform tool belt that can support your organization's growth. Use your analytics to contribute to your bottom line so that you can grow your efforts (and your budget).

CHAPTER FOUR

FIVE STEPS TO START RIGHT NOW

CHAPTER CONTRIBUTOR: CHRIS VAUGHAN

We need a lot more transparency without sacrificing marketing performance, and consumers deserve a choice, but the solutions aren't black and white. There's more nuance than that. Performance and privacy can and should coexist. It's not a zero-sum game, and you now have the tools, processes, and frameworks to achieve competitive advantage in a way that respects consumers' privacy.

People created businesses and products to serve the needs of individuals, not the other way around. We need to serve our consumers, and they want respect. Is the consumer at the center of your strategy? Anything that doesn't respect privacy principles will not be sustainable, whether it's your strategy or the technology you're using.

Place customers at the center of your strategy from the lens of your organization. Now it's more important than ever to centralize their privacy, not their identity. Take only what consumers freely offer you (when they understand what they are giving).

By this point, we've talked about new regulations, technical restrictions, and the platforms you'll need to keep in mind to execute these changes. Don't worry—we know what you're thinking. *That's all great in theory, but how do I actually implement these strategies?*

In this chapter, we've laid out a five-step plan to help your organization meet your privacy goals. Consider where you want to end up when it's done. During the first three months, you will make a full assessment of your company and your marketing and data-collection strategies. You need to consider the fragility of your digital stack—some of your processes are going to break and be completely dysfunctional. We need to shift our mindset to discover relevant solutions.

In the months ahead, you'll need to make many modifications. But keep in mind, everyone is experiencing the same disruption. Right now, the playing field is level. If you embrace the principles we've outlined and execute our strategy, then you will position yourself above your competitors.

Navigating the privacy-centric reality is attainable. Just take it one step at a time. Below is our strategy to protect your organization today and build your tomorrow.

In Chapter 1 we told you about a client in a hot potato situation where no one wanted to lead the charge to update their privacy policy, which led to each department passing the problem onto the next. Step one of our road map addresses this issue head-on.

STEP ONE: APPOINT A PRIVACY LEAD AND CREATE YOUR DATA GOVERNANCE COUNCIL

It's critical to define ownership of your organization's privacy initiative. You must decide who will be the decision maker and who will comprise the cross-functional team. There are considerations for whom you should include. We'll start by discussing who makes a great privacy team lead.

When decisions need to be made, consensus rarely works. In our experience, organizations that build nimble and effective data governance teams appoint someone as the team leader, with the power to approve or decline initiatives and delegate tasks. Whoever your organization appoints as the team lead will certainly have to make difficult decisions. And they won't always be the most popular person within the organization.

Your privacy lead should also be familiar with the legal and technical recommendations made by the council; however they do not need to be an expert in every nuance of data privacy. Instead, this person should know enough about the full privacy landscape to make smart decisions and rely on the privacy council to help them do so.

The team lead should be from the business side or the IT side of the organization (and not compliance, for example). Chief information officers (CIOs) generally can fulfill this role. They have both the influence within the organization to make high-level changes as well as the technical background to understand what needs to be implemented and how to do it.

The team lead won't understand every nuance of data privacy strategy. That's why you'll also need a legal representative on your council. This expert can give the team lead the insights they need to make good decisions. Marketing can create a new campaign to acquire first-party data, for example, and legal can review their plan to ensure compliance. Once the council agrees, the team lead can green-light the initiative.

As we alluded to above, the council should include internal representatives to form a cross-functional team. Effective councils we've been a part of include representatives from marketing, media, compliance (legal), and data architecture. It should also include external advisors or privacy partners. These people should be experts at data architecture, government regulations, and the current most-effective strategies that other organizations are currently using.

The biggest privacy obstacle we see organizations face is an inability to make decisions. To avoid this pitfall, ensure your council consists of the right people who can give good recommendations to the team lead. Inform them that they are not there solely to brainstorm, but to push initiatives through. Further, empower that lead to make choices and implement strategies. Create quarterly milestones to help evaluate the effectiveness of the council.

STEP TWO: PERFORM A STRATEGIC RISK ASSESSMENT

A strategic risk assessment for your business and platforms (and processes) is a critical next step. Throughout the book we've shown you examples of global organizations whose operations came to a grinding halt because they realized they were noncompliant with government regulations. Understanding the legal landscape and ensuring you aren't breaking the law is a logical first step.

While your marketing plan must pass legal, as a marketer you must also assess your company's reliance on third-party data, third-party cookies, and technologies that will no longer be effective in the privacy-focused future. If you are heavily reliant on third-party data, it's time to incorporate more first-party data strategies into your marketing plan. If your organization leverages an ad-tech platform reliant on third-party cookies for measurement, you'll need to shift to non-identifier-based approaches (such as media mix modeling).

An impact analysis is the first step in completing a strategic risk assessment. Specifically in the context of privacy-centric marketing, this must include an analysis of the location of your user base. If most of your consumers are in the European Union, for example, you must obtain explicit consent before processing personal data for advertising, significantly reducing your addressable audiences.

Another aspect of an impact analysis is understanding the technologies that are in use. We've discussed some of the technical restrictions that limit access to user identifiers. The impact analysis can give insight into how prevalent the usage of these technologies are among your customer base.

Once you understand your consumers and the technology they use, you can project which marketing and advertising activities are the most impacted (and how much is currently being invested in those areas). To do this, conduct the second stage of the strategic risk assessment, the channel analysis. The channel analysis analyzes each of your digital marketing channels and the tactics employed for audience creation, targeting, and measurement. You may find that your campaigns with the highest return on ad spend (ROAS) are targeted against audiences built with third-party data. Or that campaign optimization is reliant upon attribution models reliant upon third-party cookies. These insights will bring to light the tactics and capabilities necessary to address as you redefine your data strategy.

You'll find that some strategies are going to be more practical, while other options are less so. The best thing to do now is to begin forecasting the effects of these changes to your team and leadership so they understand the impact to the bottom line. While it's impossible to perfectly model every hypothetical change, it will allow you to effectively set expectations.

To help make the strategic risk assessment process easier, we included a free risk assessment tool in the privacy-centric marketing portal (https://infotrust.com/privacy-portal). Once you finish reading, navigate to the assessment.

STEP THREE: IDENTIFY AND MAP YOUR DATA

A parcel in the mail doesn't move directly to its destination. Instead it goes through multiple distribution centers on its way to your doorstep. Consumer data is the same way. Data mapping is the process of uncovering the sometimes-complex pathway of data.

Data mapping is useful because it informs compliance. It's a huge input for regulatory needs like privacy disclosures and opt outs, as well as architectural considerations. That's why you'll want to understand where the data comes from and where it goes as well as the mechanisms that are used for that transport. Lastly, you'll want to know why the data is being collected in the first place. It's one thing to understand the data path, but another to recognize why it is going to a specific location.

Data Map

	Capturing Consumer Data →	Storing Consumer Data →	Using Consumer Data →	Displaying Consumer Data
Consumer Data	Websites	Data Lake	Campaign Management Tools	Websites
	Mobile Apps	CDP	Personalization Engines	Mobile Apps
	IoT Devices	CRM	Dashboards	IoT Devices
	Etc.	DMP	Analytics	Etc.
		Etc.	Etc.	

© InfoTrust

Data minimization is about ensuring you only collect data you absolutely need to accomplish a defined use case. What data is necessary to continue executing at a level and pace that generates revenue? Decide whether the insights you gain from third-party sources are relevant. For those that are, determine whether there is a way to gain the same insight from other sources.

Data mapping is generally a more technical activity. Development operations teams are responsible for implementation and configuration of platforms, so they will be more familiar with the data architecture. Meanwhile, marketing can usually answer the "why" question, as in what the purpose for collection is. Pairing that knowledge should generate a full picture of the data map.

Data Flow

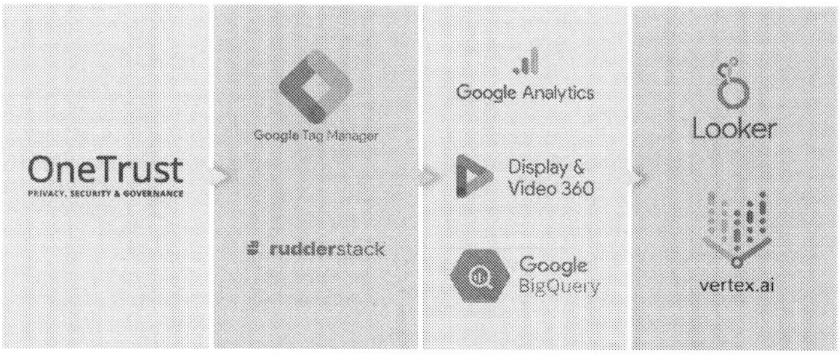

© InfoTrust

STEP FOUR: DEVELOP A PRIVACY-CENTRIC TRANSFORMATION ROAD MAP

In step two, you conducted your strategic risk assessment to identify which marketing channels—and the tactics within them—are most at risk of being negatively impacted by the changing privacy environment. Now it's time to prioritize the actions necessary to transform into a privacy-centric marketing organization. For this, you'll need a road map.

To create a customized privacy-centric transformation road map, aggregate the insights from the strategic risk assessment, highlighting the channels and tactics with the highest risk. Start by identifying data collection architecture and data enrichment capabilities that could address risks across multiple high-risk areas. Break down the people, platforms, and processes you'll need to bring these things to life and weigh them against capacity constraints across various teams.

While this can feel overwhelming, it's helpful to approach the road map with a *crawl, walk, run* mindset.

In the crawl stage (short-term, first three to six months), it's important to lay the foundation by standardizing data structures, setting up the data collection architecture for true first-party ownership, and emphasizing first-party data capture. In the walk stage (mid-term, six to twelve months), you can begin building on the foundation by testing non-cookie-reliant measurement techniques, developing more advanced first-party data analysis capabilities, and testing new ways of targeting using insights generated from first-party data. Finally in the run stage (long-term, twelve-plus months), you can begin maturing first-party data analysis via AI and machine learning, begin executing in the cookieless advertising environment through real-time audience definition, and foster a culture of continuous testing.

Your road map will be specific to your organization. What follows is an example road map based upon the outcomes of previous strategic risk assessments we have conducted with clients.

	Collection	Enrichment	Activation
Crawl 0–6 months	Emphasize email capture strategies online and offline	Design marketing data warehouse on cloud environment	Establish technical and cultural architecture for testing
	Define and collect owned user identifier	Standardize data structure and nomenclature	Activate named addressable user cohort
	Aggregate data from all platforms in canonical data object		
Walk 6–12 months	Deploy server-side data distribution across properties	Develop in-house lead scoring for audience definitions	Pilot full-funnel advertising strategy and automation
	Set and manage owned IP identifier via header response	Test identity resolution solutions	Execute tests measured via non-cookie-reliant techniques
		Conduct LTV analysis to segment users	Optimize campaigns via user-level AB testing
		Integrate marketing data sources for cross-channel analytics	Test clean-room solutions for activation channels
Run 12–24 months	Deploy server-side data distribution across properties	Expand machine learning to segment users and cater experience	Process in place for continual testing and improvement
		Enable real-time audience definitions and lead scoring	Leverage lead scoring solution for real-time audience
		Enhance goals with customer segments and value metrics	

CRAWL: SHORT-TERM, FIRST THREE TO SIX MONTHS

- Emphasize strategies for the collection of persistent user identifiers (such as email capture)
- Aggregate data needs for all platforms in a central data object on page—emphasize data minimization
- Pilot server-side data distribution solutions
- Define and collect owned first-party user identifier across all owned digital properties
- Design marketing data warehouse on organization-owned cloud environment

- Standardize data structure and nomenclature across analytics and activation platforms
- Establish technical and cultural architecture for strategic testing
- Activate named addressable user cohort in audience creation and measurement

WALK: MID-TERM, SIX TO TWELVE MONTHS

- Deploy server-side data distribution across all owned properties
- Set and manage owned first-party identifier via header response method
- Develop in-house lead scoring solution for real-time audience definitions
- Test identity resolution solutions
- Conduct LTV analysis to segment addressable users
- Integrate marketing data sources in marketing data warehouse for cross-channel analysis
- Pilot full-funnel advertising strategy and in-platform automation
- Execute tests measured via non-cookie-reliant techniques
- Test clean room solutions for activation channels
- Optimize campaigns via user-level A/B testing on named addressable user cohort

RUN: LONG-TERM, TWELVE-PLUS MONTHS

- Migrate all platforms to server-side tag management (as functionality becomes available)
- Expand machine learning to segment users and personalize their experience
- Develop capabilities to enable real-time audience definitions and lead scoring

- Enhance measurement goals with customer segments and value metrics
- Process in place for continual testing and improvements to advertising channels and digital marketing
- Leverage in-house lead-scoring solution for real-time audience definition and activation

This road map emphasizes prioritization. First identify what strategies will be most impacted (strategic risk assessment) and then rank them based on what is most important to your business. Then identify what you can begin working on tomorrow. Next, ask yourself what is predicated on other tasks being completed.

To help make the strategic risk assessment process and road map development easier, we included a free risk assessment tool in the privacy-centric marketing portal.

STEP FIVE: CHOOSE YOUR PRIVACY PARTNER

It's critically important to educate yourself on the nuances of these changes and then use that information to educate your team. Partner with privacy-focused agencies and attend relevant conferences to gain new insights on privacy-centric strategies. Stay away from companies that are trying to scare you. You should work with partners that want you to see things as they are. And while changes need to be made, your partner should view this moment as a disruptive opportunity to propel your organization forward.

Start-ups will be in a more advantageous position if they embrace the changes we're recommending. Smaller teams can make changes faster, identify a point person more quickly, and set up new processes (because all their processes are already new; they're practiced in this area).

Large enterprises can make these changes too. They just need a head start. Without it, running as soon as these changes take place will become a liability for your organization. Large businesses need to stay mindful of this competitive advantage.

You'll likely employ multiple partners. One may handle cookie consent while another may manage consumer data platforms. Still others may help advise you on how to put together or adjust your privacy road map and other privacy-related, high-level goals.

The truth is that no matter how great a council you'll build, you will need outside support. Your partner should be a strategic advisor who understands the technical and legal requirements and sits on your council to offer perspective and strategic advice. They should also have a high-level understanding of the privacy-centric landscape to help fill any gaps in your privacy plan.

To help you envision what to look for in an outside organization, we put together an easy-to-use checklist. It incorporates the elements we've deemed important in a privacy partner.

By now you understand the legal, technical, and consumer-driven landscape of the new privacy-centric reality. That means it's time to deeply assess how to collect data with compliant practices.

CHAPTER FIVE

DATA COLLECTION IN THE PRIVACY-CENTRIC REALITY

CHAPTER CONTRIBUTOR: TYLER BLATT

In his eight years at InfoTrust, Tyler has brought the concept of full-stack developer to the analytics and marketing tag world. Starting with tag implementation and finishing with data warehouse creation, he has covered the full scope of the analytics data life cycle. He is currently on the strategy team, where he uses his industry experience to determine the best way to adapt to the changing market.

In 2021, the dating app Grindr made headlines in *The New York Times*, but not in the way most companies want to. The Norwegian Data Protection Authority (DPA) found that Grindr illegally transmitted users' locations to third-party advertisers like MoPub without explicit consent. This put them in violation of European data protection law.

Despite what they called a "first in class" data protocol, Grindr was fined 100 million Norwegian kroner ($11.7 million USD) for this violation.

But the cost of this mistake was much higher than the fine, their transgression more than non-compliance. Grindr is a dating app for the LGBTQ+ community, and they were sharing the location of their users. That location was so precise that a person could theoretically track a user to a specific building. In other words, location data could potentially out a user. Even more serious, their data practices risked the safety of users in countries where consensual same-sex sexual acts are illegal or taboo.

Consider the reputational damage for a company that jeopardizes the safety of its users. Not only did Grindr incur a massive fine, but the long-term damage to their reputation is still unknown.

Grindr's approach to data protocol highlights why a strong data strategy considers factors beyond legal compliance. If Grindr had followed our next principle, they could have avoided this scandal.

Considering new regulations and consumer expectations, our second principle is as necessary as it is logical: first-party ownership of first-party data. It's a straightforward concept: organizations should collect and manage their consumers' data themselves.

If we take a closer look, this principle has two components: the acquisition of first-party data and ownership of that data. Let's start by defining what first-party data is and why it will take center stage in a privacy-centric future.

UNDERSTANDING FIRST-PARTY DATA

You're at a restaurant with a friend. The waiter comes to your table, and you order avocado toast. That order is first-party data, which is information a user directly provides or that is directly observed. The next time you visit, the waiter instead turns to your friend to ask what you would like. That's second-party data, or information supplied by a partner. On your third visit, the waiter doesn't ask either of you what you'd like, but instead just shows up with two orders of avocado toast because this is what you usually order at restaurants similar to this one. Information like this that is collected and collated from various external sources is third-party data.

Ownership of Data

Data Type	Description	Future State
Third-Party	Behavioral, interest-based, and demographic data that is collected by an external source; sometimes anonymized or aggregated	Will be less available and relied upon by organizations due to privacy regulations
Second-Party	Behavioral data collected that is another company's first-party data but can sometimes be difficult to integrate	Usage will likely depend on industry and be more limited to only be shared between trusted partners
First-Party	Data about your consumers gathered and owned by your organization; can enrich user identity or create personalized CX	Should be the primary focus of data collection as it is the most privacy-centric and durable
Zero-Party	Subset of first-party data focused on data your customer explicitly chooses to provide to your organization to add value to your relationship	Provides an opportunity to create greater touchpoints with your most loyal and engaged consumers

© InfoTrust InfoTrust

First-party data comprises two categories. The first includes user-provided information, like when a user registers with your company, provides contact information, selects preferences, or gives feedback. The second category is what behaviors can legally and directly be observed. This includes information about what that customer buys, what they view and interact with on your website, or what selections they make.

As we continue to phase out third-party data globally, first-party data becomes even more valuable to organizations.

Let's revisit our airline example where there are two passengers seated next to each other on a flight, and you spend the same number of resources to attract each.

The person who purchased the ticket through the website had to enter their birth date, credit card number, origin and destination. This means you have access to all of that information, including the cost of the ticket they purchased and other preferences that will help you market directly to them.

However, you do not get that type of information from a seat purchased through a third-party vendor because that information was not required. Without that information, it is much harder to market directly to that consumer, underscoring the importance of first-party data. One passenger will spend much more money with your company because you can tailor your interactions, while the other person may be just as willing to spend money, but you don't have the information to market to them and build a long-term relationship.

ZERO-PARTY DATA

Zero-party data is only the first-party data that is directly given. This commonly includes information like email addresses and user preferences. We won't further distinguish between the two in this book because in practice, you won't necessarily separate the two. Each is collected, stored, and acted upon in the exact same way.

To build those long-term relationships, you need data. And the best data that you can get is from a one-on-one relationship with the consumer. The customer relationship is so important. To build a strong relationship, you need to understand your consumer. Because acquisition costs are so high, you need a higher lifetime value, which piggybacks off that relationship. To get value from the consumer, you need to be delivering value to them over time. The more information you have about them and their preferences, the better you can do that.

Let's dive deeper into collecting first-party data.

© marketoonist.com

WHAT IS FIRST-PARTY DATA WORTH TO YOU?

Do you overpay for first-party data? Most organizations are so eager to collect it that they end up overpaying through discounts and promo codes. This is problematic for so many reasons. First, it's expensive. Not only is there less revenue, but it cheapens the overall perception of your brand. If your product is always on sale, the sale price effectively becomes the retail price. After a while, customers start to feel ripped off if they pay full price for a product they usually get at a discount.

Sometimes that would still make first-party data worth the price... that is, if it was accurate. How much is an email address from a throwaway account worth to you? It's arguably worth negative dollars when you consider the cost to acquire and store that data.

What if you could create a world where your users enthusiastically give you accurate information? Their main email address, accurate demographic information, and their genuine preferences are high-quality data sets. And this information comes from building a long-term trusting relationship with them.

You're a marketer, but you're also a consumer. How often do you give brands your throwaway email address to receive 10 percent off? How often do you give them an address you regularly check?

Clearly, not all first-party data is of the same quality. We'll show you how to encourage self-identification earlier in the sales process by exchanging something of value like access to exclusive content, member perks, and great user experience. These create a direct line of communication to your self-identified brand audience.

Building a long-term relationship with customers is an incredibly cost-effective way to acquire more first-party data. If your customers already know, love, and trust your brand, they will want to answer questions and help build a better experience. This is the kind of insight that money alone can't buy—and the best part is that you don't have to pay for it.

COLLECTING FIRST-PARTY DATA

Collecting first-party data has to be easy and straightforward for everyone involved. On the marketing side, collection may even be easier than in the past. You decide what data you want to collect, create a value exchange, and then ask for it.

However, many brands fail to capture data because it's cumbersome or complicated for the user to input. When this happens, the user decides the value exchange is no longer in their favor. Consider user-centricity and the grandma test at all levels of the consumer experience. Remember the airport Wi-Fi example from earlier? It wasn't just that the connection was slow, but also that it was difficult to input data in an unfamiliar language.

In the last section, we discussed that organizations acquire first-party data through long-term relationships with customers. That idea can fully be explored when we consider prolonging collection over a longer timeline. Brands like Amazon are successful in part because they collect information about ongoing purchases. It continues to expand their understanding of who you are as a buyer. And if that understanding doesn't happen, the relationship dissolves.

In our own relationships, we don't learn everything there is to know about someone in the first interaction, right? You don't meet a friend of a friend and know their hobbies until after you've had a conversation. You may never build the kind of relationship with them where you know one another's birthdays.

When someone buys a product from your organization, your relationship is just getting started. Then you'll send them something like an email and grow that connection. By the time that person has made their second, third, and fourth purchases, you're starting to get a feel for who they are and they are starting to understand you as a brand.

If you were to ask them to answer one or two quiz questions at the beginning of the relationship, do you think you'd get a response? If you did, do you think it's likely to be accurate information? As the relationship progresses, the chance of receiving accurate, personal information increases. In that way, you continuously expand user profiles.

In addition to collecting first-party data, it's also time to assess your reliance on third-party data. How much remarketing or interest-based advertising against third-party audiences are you doing? If you only had your first-party data about your customer, how much would you know today?

At this stage, it's time to focus on bulking up your first-party data strategy. That being said, it's imperative to do so in a way that is sustainable and doesn't sacrifice the user experience.

OWNERSHIP OF FIRST-PARTY DATA

Many of our clients rely on Google Analytics (GA) for both user data and interaction data on websites. But as of the time of publishing, use of GA is non-compliant under the GDPR in specific cases. Despite the restrictions, marketers around the world are still very reliant on the platform for all kinds of business.

That was a major problem when in early 2022, the Austrian Data Protection Authority (DPA) ruled that a particular website's usage of GA was non-compliant. What's surprising about this specific case is that they weren't using third-party data. Rather, they were analyzing first-party data using a third party (GA) to do so.

A few weeks later, France's CNIL ruled that any use of GA in broad terms was in non-compliance with the GDPR.

Soon, we (InfoTrust) received hundreds of emails.

Is Google Analytics illegal?

What can we use instead?

Can we just change the way we use the platform?

The short-term answer depended on where in the world the company asking was based and the location of its customers. After the Austrian DPA ruling, many organizations responded by simply tweaking the way they used the platform and quit using specific identifiers.

But when France's much broader ruling came out, the companies that used GA were concerned. All of their data was stored on a platform France and Austria had deemed to be non-compliant.[22] And as of the writing of this book, the final guidance across the EU is still unclear. That means the status of all their customer data is in the air.

This brings us back to the long-term response to third-party data. If a company is using GA in a compliant way, there is no reason to stop using it. It's reasonable to expect GA to build and implement new technologies to make it easier for brands to continue to use the platform. But these cases reveal the impor-

---

22 "Partial Decision, European Center for Digital Rights," NOYB, October 2, 2020, https://noyb.eu/sites/default/files/2022-01/E-DSB%20-%20Google%20Analytics_EN_bk.pdf. "Use of Google Analytics and data transfers to the United States: the CNIL orders a website manager/operator to comply," CNIL, published February 10, 2022, https://www.cnil.fr/en/use-google-analytics-and-data-transfers-united-states-cnil-orders-website-manageroperator-comply.

tance of owning the full data supply chain. Without a crystal ball, you'll never be able to predict with complete certainty what will and will not be illegal in the future.

Ultimately, the legal responsibility to be compliant falls on the organization. And it's also their responsibility to accomplish business goals. With those two things in mind and with respect to the current legal climate, the only surefire way to meet both requirements is through first-party ownership of first-party data.

First-party data is also an essential component of any risk management strategy. The ability to store and analyze the data yourself minimizes risk across the board. Consider the vulnerability of storing that data you worked so hard to gather with an intermediary. They could easily go out of business due to a regulatory change or could suffer a data breach. As personal information becomes more expensive, so too does it become riskier to entrust it to others.

To truly understand your users and really pull insights from the data in the next chapter, it's a prerequisite to have as complete and accurate information as possible. If your inputs are inaccurate, your outputs are also going to be inaccurate. You might be developing insights, but they are completely off base.

The other issue is related to accuracy and consistency. We have information about our users' interactions in a number of different places. We have our customer relationship management (CRM) system where we have the actual user information. We have our web analytics platforms where we have interaction information. We have our e-commerce systems where we have transaction information.

Traditionally, most organizations rely on third parties to provide each of those different services. Each third party has their own standards or recommended methods for data structure and how things should be implemented. If you have different structures, different taxonomies, and different naming conventions across each of those different platforms, it makes integration for that single view of the consumer really difficult, if not impossible.

Relying on third parties and their standards is not necessarily in your best interest. So when we talk about ownership, we're really talking about not just owning the data and flows to mitigate the compliance risk, but also about owning the standards, taxonomies, and naming conventions that are being used across all of your systems. That then provides a foundation for you to be able to integrate these first-party data sets to do more analysis, better understand your users, and generate more insights, which we can then activate on.

Retailers naturally collect lots of information about their consumers. They observe when customers go to the store or website, browse items, all the way up to completing the purchase (and whether that's done online or at a brick-and-mortar store). They might also collect an email for that person, but then they're not able to bring that data together because, often, this type of information lives in different databases or different data sets. Those retailers are either not able to analyze it, or don't really understand the full picture of their consumers' behavior because they treat them as non-connected users. Retailers do not have the ability, for example, to see that the same person buys certain products online and then buys certain products offline. They can't see the time differences between online browsing and online purchases versus doing it in store.

Customer lifetime value is a big deal in the past, present, and future. With this segmented information, it is practically impossible to have a true calculation. The value of a consumer is obvious, regardless of where they're transacting. If we're unable to link that information together, we cannot get to true value and don't know who our most valuable consumers are. Therefore we cannot develop our strategies around finding similar customers.

LEVERAGING SECOND-PARTY DATA IN THE PRIVACY ERA

Second-party data is a direct partner's first-party data that they are providing to another party. For example, platforms like Google and Facebook have a lot of first-party data about their users, from what they browse to their email address. If one of those platforms then shared that information with your organization, that would make it second-party data.

You can use second-party data to gain a fuller picture of path-to-purchase. For example, with the deprecation of third-party cookies, you no longer have visibility into what your consumers are doing outside your ecosystem. So if you spent $10 million on display advertisements, you now have no clue which ads were viewed more frequently on other platforms.

But if you are heavily investing in a partner like Google or Facebook, you can marry *your* conversion information with *their* impression information. In that way, you now know which ads get more clicks and which ones resulted in a conversion.

Like the example above, brands trying to evaluate the effectiveness of their marketing efforts can leverage second-party data to gain insight they may have learned through third-party platforms in the past. Brands who advertise with a large publisher, like a search engine, social platform, or specific website, can take their first-party data to that second party and effectively compare notes. This is done using shared identifiers from the two parties and consented user data.

For example, it's possible to upload the data of your website users and then go to Google to find out whether they've been on their platform. Considering the popularity of Google, it's likely they have. Of course, you can do this with any partner. By combining those two data sets, you can better understand the full journey of users who purchase your products. In a later chapter we'll dive deeper into second-party data strategies. But for now, recognize that in this new world, you'll learn to creatively leverage the tools at your disposal to gain insight.

THE FUTURE OF THIRD-PARTY DATA

If you respect your users, it's unlikely that third-party data will have a place in your strategy moving forward. However there are a few instances where it may still be possible to use it in a compliant and effective way.

One of our clients works in the industrial product space. They use third-party data in the form of weather information to supplement their user segment information. For example, if a major storm disrupts an area, they'll overlay that information over their data set to target users who most likely need a specific set of their products, like siding or roofing materials.

In this way, the future of third-party data means using it to gain supplemental, contextual information that respects user privacy. Other potential strategies include social listening, or scanning social media platforms for conversations related to your industry. Social listening enables marketers to understand what people are talking about in a particular region.

A pharmaceutical company's creative way to use third-party data in the privacy era is to target areas with higher cases of influenza with messaging around the flu vaccine. They do not target anyone specifically based on their flu status, but rather certain profiles of people who are in a high-case region.

It's possible that third-party data will still have a compliant role in your data strategy. However, you can expect to rely on it less heavily than before, using it to add context to first- and second-party data.

Now that you understand what data to collect, it's time to optimize storage and collection.

OPTIMIZING DATA STORAGE

To understand how to best optimize your data storage strategy, let's look at a simple matrix that explores the data being stored. All user data can be separated into four categories: consented, non-consented, registered, and non-registered. Based on those categories, we can then group data accordingly.

	REGISTERED	NON-REGISTERED
CONSENTED	Named Addressable	Pseudonymous
NON-CONSENTED	Named Non-addressable	Anonymous

Quadrant one houses users who are registered (likely via email) and have consented to being tracked, making them both **named**

and addressable. This means they have consented and given their email to the company, so marketers know who they are and can advertise to them directly.

Quadrant two includes non-registered users who have consented to being tracked, making them pseudo-anonymous, or **pseudonymous.** These users haven't provided their email to the company, but have consented so marketers can still identify them on their owned and operated digital properties via a first-party cookie.

Quadrant three holds registered, non-consented users who are **named and non-addressable.** This means they have provided an identifier to receive communication, but only in a limited capacity (such as signing up for a newsletter) while denying tracking and advertising permissions.

The last quadrant shows non-registered and non-consented users, which makes them **anonymous.** These are the people who do not provide any persistent identifier and do not want any of their personal data used for advertising.

It's imperative to collect data from every group listed. Certainly you'll have the most insight available concerning those that are named and addressable, but that doesn't mean there isn't value in the other groups. However, it's best to store information on each group separately within your data warehouse for analysis. That way if a user sends a deletion request, you can easily delete their personal data without compromising the rest of the data set.

Imagine the groups as a triangle built on anonymous data. The anonymous data set is the base because it is foundational for a holistic view of consumer behavior. It includes impersonal data like campaign tracking parameters, time of day, web page interactions or app clicks and impressions, and transactions (without any identifying information). The aggregate data that this contributes to allows you to gain insights like what campaigns bring the most traffic, which products are most popular, and what content is most effective at driving conversions. With these insights you'll use anonymous data to make large-scale marketing decisions that are perfectly compliant.

The middle of the triangle is composed of the pseudonymous group. This data set comprises information from users who allow unique first-party device identifiers to be collected alongside the anonymous interaction information but do not disclose contact information. This group is very valuable because you can see which ad brought a user to the site, learn which page they landed on, and use the identifier to tie together interactions throughout their visit to the site all the way to conversion.

The tip of the triangle comprises information from users who are named and addressable. For this user group, you can continue targeted marketing via the persistent identifier, understand behavior cross-device and over time, and generate deep insights about your high-value users.

The Data Triangle

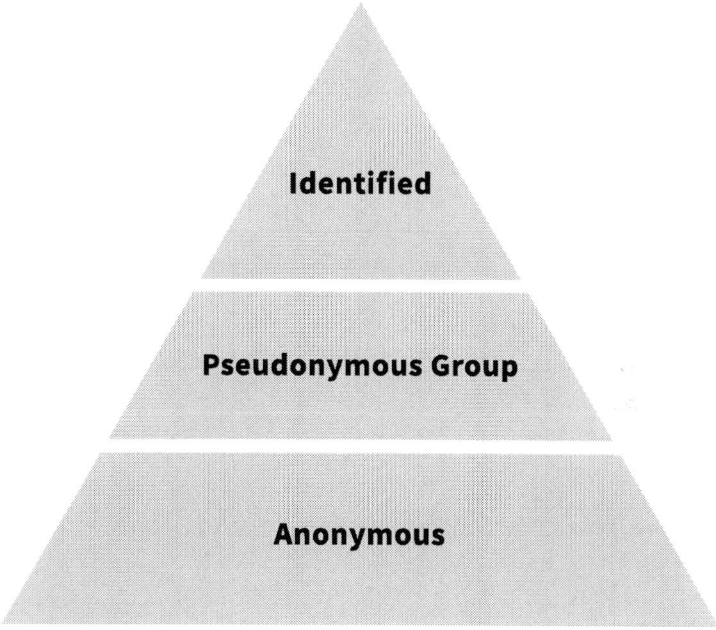

© InfoTrust

By separating the data sets, you ensure that your organization can fulfill deletion requests easily, without accidentally deleting information you are not obligated to. If a user fills out a deletion request, you can now simply delete the personal information, without deleting the anonymous data, too.

Unfortunately, existing third-party storage solutions do not partition user data in the way described above. So what do you do? We suggest designing your own first-party marketing data warehouse with a collection system you own so that you can collect compliantly in a way that respects the privacy of all of your users.

DATA DISTRIBUTION

A tag management system (TMS) is a software that distributes data collected on your site to different platforms (such as Facebook, Google, Amazon, Twitter, and Snapchat) so that you don't have to add code for each directly on your website. There are two types of TMS: client side and server side.

Client-side tag management distributes the data directly from the customer's computer. Traditionally, data collection existed entirely on the client side. This was the path of least resistance. Why build server-side tech when it was easier and cheaper to process all that data client-side?

There are a few issues with client-side TMS. For one, you can't control how code runs on someone else's computer, which means things like ad blockers (which only work on code run client-side) or just people messing with their computers can lead to inaccurate and incomplete data. Second, third-party cookies require client-side scripts to set and access them. The deprecation of third-party cookies removes this need, meaning there will soon no longer be a compelling reason to run client-side TMS.

With the value of client-side TMS decreasing, many companies are going to swing to server-side TMS platforms. **Server-side tag management** sends data first to a cloud environment where the distribution then occurs from. This allows you to execute how the code runs in the cloud and gives you full control of what data is sent where.

Further, all of the interactive elements of the web relied heavily on JavaScript (think buttons, login windows, and pop-ups). JavaScript is everywhere, but it isn't secure because its code allows for piggybacking, which is when secret extra code is loaded on top of the code you sent to the customer's computer. As information bounces between sites on a computer, you have no control of what gets piggybacked onto third-party code and where it sends the data. Not only is this a security problem, but it creates a privacy problem too. If a user requests you delete all of their information, you might not even know where you've sent all their information. If you don't know, you can't effectively comply.

With a server-side TMS, everything is kept in a black box. You control all of the code dictating the data collection and distribution, so it's far more secure and accurate. This is what's going to allow you to design a system that separates your named, consented, and anonymous user data. And instead of using third-party pixels like Google or Facebook to send data and compromising your ownership of it, you have first-party ownership of the full process.

To be clear, Google Analytics will still work with a server-side setup. In fact, it's actually *even more reliable*. Using server-side, you can enforce data standards and taxonomies much more effectively. The difference is that instead of running the third-party tag or script on your website and that info being sent directly to Google, the data is sent to your server and you determine what to send to Google.

Once you've defined your data model and chosen your storage, you need a server-side mechanism to collect data in real time.

DATA COLLECTION

Server-side tag management can do all the things your client-side code was doing, but also allows you to leverage the data that's already flowing through your collection architecture to feed third-party platforms and, in addition, drop the information in your owned database.

This prevents issues of ownership and enables situations like backfilling data. For example, if you onboard a new platform, ideally you will send all of your historical data to that platform. That's only possible if you own all the historical data. You no longer need to rely on third-party platforms for reporting or to grant you permission to use old data because you will always have your own version in your owned database.

This allows you to evaluate how platforms are actively affecting your business beyond the measurement capability. If third parties aren't responsible for storage and measurement, then what are you paying them for? While you do have to invest in the infrastructure to create this model and database yourself, it's an investment in your long-term gain that decays over time (meaning it doesn't cost more money later), unlike platforms that can continue to increase prices for their services over time.

Decoupling from reliance on third-party capabilities empowers you to collect, store, and own data in a way that is compliant and respects the privacy preferences of your users while still allowing you to activate it in your business strategy. As a company, it's your responsibility to figure out how third parties can elevate what you already have at your disposal. We don't suggest relying on them to take care of the basics for you in this changing environment, but they still have features to offer.

EXTRACT, TRANSFORM, LOAD (ETL)

The job of a client-side platform is basically to take all of your customers' data and send it everywhere but where you own. It sends data to platforms like Google Analytics and Facebook, but not to your first-party marketing data warehouse. Some server-side TMS offer ETL capabilities that allow you to change that by extracting the data from all the different places that the client-side platforms have sent it, transform the data into a data model that works for you (i.e., delete user IDs, format numbers and letters, etc.), and load it somewhere else (i.e., a place that you own).

Reverse-ETL

R-ETL is the concept of taking all the data that you've collected from different platforms and using it to create single customer views. Then you send those single customer views back out to the partner platforms to complete the user's data profile in each (it is important that this is only done with consented users).

OWNED FIRST-PARTY DATA WAREHOUSE

Some server-side platforms make it a point to own their own data warehouse so that if platforms like Facebook or Twitter go down temporarily, the TMS platform's data isn't compromised. If it has its own copy of the data, it can just fill in the information on the downed social platform once it's back up again.

SEGMENTATION OF USER AND INTERACTION DATA

For named addressable users, some server-side TMS platforms also become a customer data platform (CDP) that allows you to segment all of your user data and then activate via different advertising channels.

DATA HYGIENE

Often as marketers we tend to spend way too much time talking about data collection and not enough talking about the quality of data you already have. Companies spend millions and millions of dollars on collecting data. But even if your data is well integrated and you have an amazing data warehouse, you've still created virtually zero value for your business. Any type of analysis that you do is only going to be as valuable as the quality of your inputs.

If you rely solely on a garden for your produce, chances are you'll be careful to prepare your soil and plant the right seeds. When you can't get your veggies from other sources, self-reliance is the only option. Likewise, because you will work with less data from fewer sources, you will have to take much better care of what you do have. And your data is only as clean as you keep it.

Since the information that you have access to is limited, you need to optimize and maximize it. You do that by respecting users' privacy, having a strong relationship with your users, and providing a fair value exchange.

If you follow those guidelines, more users will want to provide you with more information about their preferences. Then, because you have ownership of the entire data supply chain, you'll be able to collect that information in a consistent, uniform, and complete way.

There are many facets of the data supply chain to evaluate when considering data hygiene. For example, pieces of the chain include data collection, validation, storage, integration, monitoring, visualization, and analysis. And any imperfections or weaknesses throughout the supply chain are going to negatively impact the consumer experience (or even violate regulations).

KEY TAKEAWAYS

First-party data ownership is imperative because it reduces business risk, compliance risk, and legal risk. First-party ownership allows for visibility over exactly what data is collected, where it's stored, and how it's processed. When you have end-to-end ownership, you also have audit trails to understand exactly what information went where. It provides the foundation for you to develop uniform standards, which enables that integration critical to deriving insights. You're able to also enforce better accuracy and completeness by owning the whole process.

Historically, not everyone has prioritized first-party data. Regardless of your current practices, you'll need to emphasize ownership in the future. If you start collecting data tomorrow, you have data that starts tomorrow. If you sit on this and start in a month, well guess what happens? You have one month less data. When the rest of the world catches up, you'll have a lot more competition in that space.

Having great data by itself doesn't mean much, though it is important because otherwise you aren't going to have anything to work with. Only collecting and owning data creates zero value for your business. Having data does not mean that you have a great or strong relationship with your consumer.

Data collection is where the work starts. You have to listen, understand, and act. And once you do, you'll uncover the best path forward for you and your organization.

CHAPTER SIX

UNCOVER INSIGHTS AND TAKE ACTION WITH YOUR DATA IN A PRIVACY-CENTRIC WORLD

CHAPTER CONTRIBUTOR: PAM CASTRICONE

Pam Castricone is Head of Data Science at InfoTrust. She helps e-commerce retailers and CPG organizations uncover greater insights and value from their data assets. Specializing in statistical and machine learning models, she applies these advanced analytical techniques to drive better ROI for her clients. As a Google Cloud Certified Professional Data Engineer, Pam also helps her clients productionalize their models in the cloud to drive long-term usability and success.

Pam is also an adjunct professor at the University of Cincinnati's Lindner College of Business, where she teaches a graduate-level course on digital analytics. When she isn't analyzing data, Pam enjoys reading, the arts, and going out for brunch.

Before the changes to the privacy landscape, marketers had a lot of options for gaining insights about their customers and using those insights for personalized targeting. Let's say you are in the market for new sneakers, so you hop on Nordstrom's site and browse online. You then decide to see if any competitor sites offer something in a similar style, but a little less expensive. Nordstrom retargets you, so for the next month, those sneakers follow you around from site to site. Retargeting campaigns like these are reliant on persistent identifiers that are associated with a user. Wherever consumers go, whatever actions they take, items they buy, articles they read—all of those different behaviors are associated with an ID that represents them as a person.

Now, at some point, somebody on the Nordstrom marketing team says, "Well, that's great, but the person was just browsing for sneakers. That doesn't mean they are going to buy them. We need more information."

So on top of that data, organizations fold in additional information. Some of the largest data brokers, for example, have purchase history, credit information, credit history information, and even location data for sale. Companies can purchase online and offline behavior of an individual and then add all of that into their profiles.

An organization can quickly get to the point where they know that an individual likes to read the politics section on CNN, subscribes to *The New York Times*, lives in Minneapolis, Minnesota, has a high credit rating, recently purchased a vehicle, and is in the market to purchase a new pair of sneakers based on their browsing online. That's some serious insight.

So now Nordstrom or a third party can aggregate all of that data to look for trends. They just might learn that people with a specific credit score and zip code are 20 percent more likely to buy sneakers similar to theirs.

Now they continue to remarket to only a small group of people, making their ad even more targeted. They do not waste money on running ads to people who cannot afford that product or live in an area where they are unlikely to buy.

So why are we telling you all this? Because it demonstrates that there was a lot more happening behind the scenes than the use of clever tech. Yes, third-party data and persistent identifiers across sites are going away, but the job of marketing is still the same. Collect data, then act based on insights learned. It's not like you no longer have any data to collect, it's just that it's going to look a little different and there will be less of it, which means you'll need a new methodology to perform an analysis.

Today, it's not so simple.

NEW WORLD MARKETING

You might believe that one way to stay competitive in this more recent targeting environment lies with the actual technology platforms that are sitting in the middle. Marketers might ask: what remarketing partner can you work with that has the largest reach (i.e., present on the most websites)? Who has access to the most ad inventory so you can cast a wide net for wherever your users are going? What other third parties and data brokers have the largest pool of users and profiles that overlap with your identifiers or identifiers available to you?

But the thing is, everyone has access to those same platforms. You don't truly have a competitive advantage if you all have access to the same cookie pools and the same partners. In that market, it comes down to who can pay the most. It's a race to the bottom.

Marketers can gain an advantage by mining the information that they do have access to, which is owned first-party data. Given the changes to privacy, it's in their best interest to use newer, more privacy-focused methods to pull a lot of insights about who their most valuable users are so that they can use resources wisely.

We believe if you focus on the insights you can get from your own data, you'll derive better information. And if you have a stronger relationship with your users, you'll have more information to use. That's why it's worthwhile to internally develop capabilities for mining those insights, a more robust structure, ownership, and control of your first-party data, because it leads to—you guessed it—better insights.

For those valuable users that we want to develop a stronger relationship with, it's strategic to know what they are interested in and how we can best serve them. Then we can apply these insights to know how we can serve the entire cohort of others like them. If we know that our high-value users are really interested in a particular type of content, then we can advertise against that content and be more contextual in nature.

Consider the person buying shoes who placed them in their cart but didn't buy. In the future, the only universal way you'll be able to show a personalized ad referencing what that specific user left behind is to capture a first-party identifier like their email. This means that for retargeting campaigns, your addressable audience will be a much smaller proportion of what it was before. This underscores the importance of having consumers' loyalty and getting them to provide you their information and preferences. So while you might not be able to target unknown users in the same way, you can still deliver personalization to members of your loyalty program.

But do you really need to know the specific action of a specific user and target them individually? What if you could cast a specialized, yet wider net? In the new privacy-centric reality, you'll need to learn the characteristics of users who typically purchase your product based on first-party data.

For example, let's say Nordstrom has identified a particular cohort of users that typically spends 30 percent more with the brand. Based on their purchase history, Nordstrom also learns that the cohort is disproportionately interested in a particular line of slacks. Based on insights from their first-party data, they also identify that most of those users come from *Vanity Fair*'s and *GQ*'s websites. Now Nordstrom knows where their most valuable customers hang out and are most likely to view their ads.

We understand that you are accustomed to more precise identification technology. But it's still not clear whether consumers appreciated all that precision. Often, when we speak at conferences and ask how many are thrilled about the marketing experience, few people raise their hands. Even those who are responsible for that very same marketing admit that the experience isn't great on the consumer side. Often consumers see ads for products they already purchased or for products they aren't looking to buy.

TYPES OF USERS AND ANALYSIS

Out of the four data sets described in the last chapter, digital marketing as we know it today was built primarily on the pseudonymous quadrant. Up to this point, marketers haven't needed consumers to identify themselves to advertise to them. But with ever-growing concerns about privacy, that's quickly changing. All signs indicate that it won't be long before we need all users to be named and addressable to target them in a one-to-one manner.

One strategy might be to get the entire pseudonymous group moved to the named addressable cohort. But even if you could transfer the entire group (which isn't going to happen), that still neglects marketing to the largest group of users: anonymous. Most marketers today recognize the value of including a variety of strategies in their portfolio of campaigns targeting both pseudonymous and known users; a singular focus on the named addressable cohort will leave a sizable gap in their ability to reach customers.

In the current environment, many marketers consider anonymous data useless, but we will show you that it isn't. This mindset comes from the early days of internet marketing. The internet was young, and we weren't nearly as good with technology yet. So anonymous data was largely unhelpful at that time.

But now we have far better technology and a better understanding of data science at our disposal. We have artificial intelligence and machines built for analysis that can do a lot with anonymous data to help push non-consented users toward customer engagement. By not utilizing these tools, you're leaving data (and therefore insights and money) on the table. Shifting to a privacy-centric strategy includes utilizing all of the data available to you while still respecting user preferences.

HYBRID ADVERTISING METHOD

We are living in a hybrid environment that contains both users who are willing to share their data and users who are not. Fortunately, the problem hints at the solution—that is, a hybrid world requires a hybrid method. While cookie-based approaches to targeting won't be enough anymore, you also don't have to invent a brand-new form of advertising. You can use the original techniques from the early days of the internet and incorporate contextual advertising into your new strategy.

Instead of trying to move all of your users to the named and addressable quadrant, you want to focus on improving your relationship with consumers so that you can heighten your engagement with customers, even those who don't want you using their data for targeting. Investing in systems and architectures that enable you to operate with a blend of contextual and targeted advertising is the key to accomplishing this.

UNCOVERING INSIGHTS WITH DATA MODELING

Operating on a privacy-centric strategy revolves around collecting data with a purpose. Instead of collecting and storing as much data as possible because you can, ensure you have a good reason for every piece of data you collect and store. This leads to only collecting data that serves you, which comes with several benefits:

- There is less overhead to maintain and store data. Being mindful of the data you maintain ensures the quality of the data you're using to generate insights is good, freeing you from the common "garbage in, garbage out" trap and reducing the amount of storage needed.
- It's consistent with the principle of data minimization. There is no reason to collect data that isn't useful. Further, having less data makes it easier to protect.
- It respects users' privacy. This means the data your customers do let you collect is more likely to have a fair value exchange.

An intentional data set is easier for analysts and data scientists to work with. Data preparation is typically the most labor-intensive portion of a modeling project, so reducing the number of fields that need to be analyzed and evaluated prior to inclusion in a model cuts down the time to insight and action. We recommend starting with a minimum viable product (MVP) model to benchmark performance and consciously adding more data and complexity as needed. By starting small, you'll be ready to test your models sooner and will more quickly identify what's working and what's not. As we will discuss later, a culture of testing and optimization is key to adapting your strategies to the new world of marketing.

Now let's talk about the actual analysis and insight you can get from your data.

MODELING WITH NAMED ADDRESSABLE USERS

For the named users who have consented to tracking, you can continue targeting users in a one-to-one personalized way. We suggest doing so with a focus on thoroughly mining this data set for learnings that can then be applied to unconsented users (as an example, you could look for particular user actions or purchasing habits that can be interpreted as signals of a potential high-value user).

One way of doing this is to create single customer views to deepen your understanding of your high-value users. This means bringing together data from across multiple systems like your website, app, and offline interactions to create as complete a picture of your relationship with an individual as possible. Let's look at some of the models that can be built and activated using data from named consented users.

© marketoonist.com

CUSTOMER LIFETIME VALUE (CLV) MODELING

This modeling technique looks at customers' past purchasing behavior and uses that data to predict their future purchases and spend. Not all customers are equally valuable to your business and by analyzing the purchase habits of your customer base, you can gain visibility into which customers are likely to be the most valuable over the entire course of their relationship with your brand.

Customer Lifetime Value Model

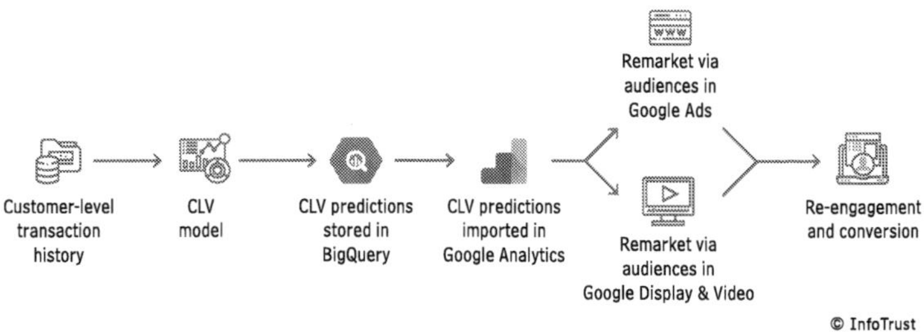

We find that CLV modeling tends to be underutilized by businesses. Even those who do look at the data typically don't use it to its fullest potential. But the high-value customers identified by a CLV model should be an important pillar of your marketing strategy because they're already engaged with your brand, and you want to keep them that way. We suggest using your insights from this data to nurture your relationships with these customers through strategies like personalization in marketing and loyalty programs.

Something to keep in mind when creating this data model is that it's intended for long-term gain. CLV is most effective when used as part of a larger customer-centric strategy that prioritizes the needs and desires of the most valuable customers across the organization.

PROPENSITY MODELING

Propensity modeling is a technique to predict which users are going to convert in the near future. While the CLV model focuses on analyzing the behavior of your customers over their entire lifetime with your brand, a propensity model produces short-term insights. The goal of this model is typically to help you nudge users who seem like they're close to conversion.

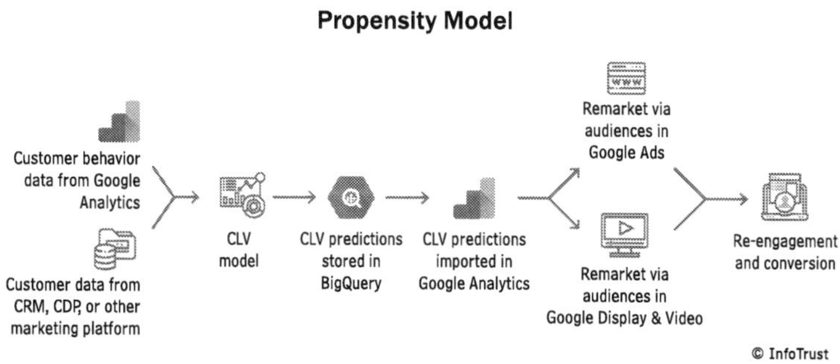

The most common way to activate a propensity model is to use it to create an audience for a retargeting campaign. The model will often uncover insights such as specific behaviors or combinations of behaviors that signal that a customer is ready to convert. For example, you may find that adding an item to a cart is a strong predictor of purchasing in the next seven days. If that action hasn't converted to a sale, you can reach out to the named addressable user with an email that says, "You left this item in your cart. Buy it before it's gone!" That's a simplistic example, but this model can be used with more sophisticated methods of detecting if a user is close to conversion as well.

TIME-TO-REORDER MODELING

Time-to-reorder modeling involves taking data on the purchase history of all your customers and using it to determine an estimated time window for when your customer should be ready for their next purchase. For example, if a skin-care brand sells a jar of moisturizer, the brand's data scientists can use a time-to-reorder model to understand how much time typically elapses between purchases and when is the optimal time to reach out to a customer to nudge them to place their next order. For example, if the purchase data indicates that customers typically buy a new jar every 120 days, then the marketing team can then track the time it's been since a named consented user's last purchase and send them a life-cycle campaign ad (e.g., a "time to reorder" email) when that person is close to the 120-day mark.

MODELING WITH PSEUDONYMOUS USERS

Users who are pseudonymous (consented but have not provided a persistent identifier) are a bit harder to target for marketing because you don't have persistent personal identifiers for them, but their consent to measurement is still valuable because you can assign your own pseudonymous identifiers to them and use insights from first-party data to personalize your ads. Plus you can combine this data set with the named addressable users to provide personalization for both groups of users. This personalization can entail a lot of things, but two strong techniques are dynamic content and product recommendations. Additionally, you can use this data to improve the customer experience by analyzing the user journey.

DYNAMIC CONTENT

If you have data on the types of content that a pseudonymous user has been interested in in the past or other relevant details about them, you can adapt the content of your website in key places to reflect the user's interests or be particularly relevant to them. For example, with access to the geographical location of consented users (pseudonymous), you can tailor the products or content displayed on the home screen of the website or app based on the local weather, such as rain gear for a user browsing from within a city where it's raining at that moment.

PRODUCT RECOMMENDATION ENGINES

Product recommendation engines are a common technique that you probably already know of because it's effective. If you have data on the products that a user has previously expressed interest in and the outcomes of behaviors exhibited by other consented users, you can better recommend related products to them that they might want to purchase, which can lead to larger basket sizes and average order value (AOV).

UNDERSTANDING THE USER JOURNEY

With pseudonymous user data, you can also analyze the sequences of user actions to uncover which interactions led to a conversion and which didn't. This analysis is great for understanding if your users are following the experience that you designed for them and identifying opportunities for improvement. For example, you may find that users are more likely to convert after interacting with a virtual try-it-on module, leading you to hypothesize that including the module on more pages would produce higher conversion rates. You could then run an A/B test to test this hypothesis and measure the value of making this change to the website or app.

MODELING WITH ANONYMOUS USERS

This data set includes all behavioral information from users but without any identifiers (persistent nor pseudonymous). While non-consented users can't be identified in any way, interaction data collected from them still offers a lot of value to analyses done on aggregate data. Even without data on sequential user interactions, you can use the anonymous interaction data to make predictions and generate valuable insights.

FORECASTING

This technique refers to looking at data that's collected at regular intervals over time and using it to predict what will happen in the future. These models are very commonly used and can give you a tremendous amount of visibility into any metric of interest.

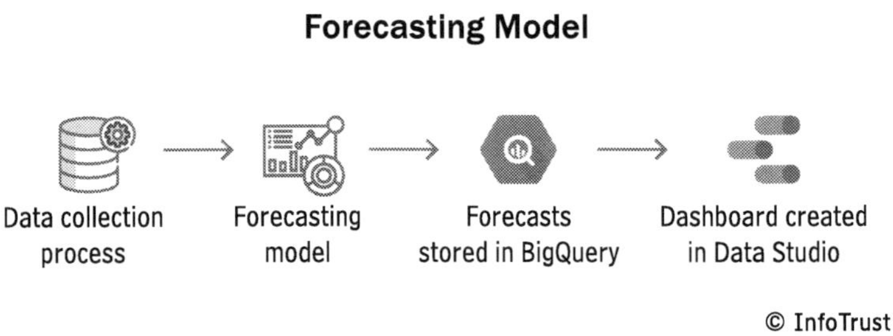

For example, we have built forecast engines for our clients that forecast revenue on an hourly basis. One of the key uses for those is during the holiday period (or other important promotional times) to provide visibility into whether the brand is on track to hit their sales targets. Using aggregate data in a forecast model lets you know much sooner if you are or aren't on track, which gives you more time to adjust your strategy if needed. This is an invaluable capability that isn't offered by analytics platforms like Google Analytics, so if you're not already doing this in-house or with another partner, we strongly suggest you consider doing so.

REGRESSION-BASED ATTRIBUTION

Regression-based attribution is an adaptation of traditional media mix modeling (MMM) that is focused on digital marketing. These models provide attribution insights from data collected in aggregate and can be used for campaign planning and budget optimization. Regression-based attribution models work best when they incorporate a number of different signals in aggregate and associate them with actual conversions to attribute value to each of the different advertising actions. For example, you can use the model to predict how changes in ad spend for particular channels or tactics will affect sales.

Regression-based attribution is important because current multi-touch attribution models rely heavily on cookie data. With the deprecation of third-party cookies and the technology changes affecting first-party cookies, the ability to use multi-touch attribution models to attribute sales to different campaigns is going to become less effective over time. Because critical campaign investment decisions are dependent on this information, we recommend getting started with a regression-based attribution model now to get comfortable with a new approach to answering those critical questions about campaign performance.

It should be noted that all of these techniques are still just models—they're not infallible in the predictions they indicate. To make the best decisions for your marketing budget, you have to test the insights.

INSIGHT TESTING

In our experience, companies extract the most value from their modeling and analysis projects when they are supported by an internal culture of testing and are dedicated to cultivating a learning-oriented mindset.

A key part of this culture includes having realistic expectations when you conduct your experiments. Expect that fewer than 50 percent of tests will produce the desired results—and that's okay! What matters is ensuring you can fail fast so that when the results don't work out, you can move on to testing the next solution quickly until you find one that works.

This is another reason we suggest starting with an MVP-type approach. It's a quick way to get feedback with few factors in play when trying to diagnose the cause of unsuccessful test results. If the results are successful, you can deploy the model to production and get started on the next problem to solve. If not, find out why. Did the governance fail? Is more data needed? Was it incorrect to assume we could apply our learnings from the named addressable users to the pseudonymous and anonymous cohorts? These are the questions everyone has right now as we adjust to a privacy-centric market. No one has all the answers yet, so the faster you find them for yourself, the better your competitive advantage will be.

CHAPTER SEVEN

PRIVACY-CENTRICITY FOR YOUR INDUSTRY

So far we've emphasized the critical elements of a privacy-centric strategy that are universal. There isn't a business in existence that wouldn't benefit from respecting the privacy of their users, owning their first-party data, and taking action based on insight. Every organization will get ahead of the competition by implementing the 6 "P"s of Data Analytics Transformation in Chapter Three. And the technologies and solutions provided in the preceding chapters are applicable to any industry.

Consider the information so far in this book as the ingredients to the recipe. Now that you have them at your disposal, it's time to use them to create your own unique dish. Every organization will apply our principles in varying degrees to build their privacy strategy. This chapter explores how you can use what you've learned in a practical way, tailored to your needs.

However, some advice is universal across industries. You'll find that in every vertical, we propose emphasizing user experience. At first glance, that may seem out of scope for a book on data privacy. But we're not talking about user experience to increase conversions. Rather, we recognize that without access to third-party cookies, organizations must value first-party data even more highly than before. And the best way to ensure high-quality first-party data is to create a flawless user experience. In this way, improved user experience is a data collection strategy.

To improve the user experience, sometimes organizations need to look outside their own vertical to find inspiration. It's possible that another industry has already found the solution to your greatest problem. And it's worth this exploration because consumers have come to expect similar user experience across verticals.

For example, the direct-to-consumer industry has made automated personalization standard across organizations. You receive a notification if you leave items in your cart and websites remember your size when browsing. And yet the financial and health industries have broadly failed to introduce that kind of experience. You may even still get a paper card with a handwritten note with your next appointment date. Wherever you are lacking, don't be afraid to look for solutions outside your competition.

We won't address every industry we work with in this chapter. However we do focus on areas we have the most expertise in. This isn't a broad sweep, but instead an in-depth exploration into the industries that we are extremely familiar with. To get the most from this chapter, look for your specific industry in the headings. If you don't see it listed, look for the closest approximation. And for even more detailed advice, check out our portal.

FINANCE

CHAPTER CONTRIBUTOR: MELANIE BOWLES

Melanie Bowles has been in the digital space for over ten years working on both the agency side and client side. She has been involved with the development of digital and optimization strategies for both small and medium businesses and Fortune 500 companies across industries. Specializing in digital transformation, Melanie has been a catalyst for helping businesses increase traffic, improve customer experience, and increase conversions and revenue. Melanie is currently an Industry Team Lead at InfoTrust, where she partners with multifunctional teams to define analytics strategy, analyze data, and evaluate the business impact of digital experiences for financial, automotive, and B2B verticals.

Consumers in the finance industry *demand* transparency and data protection. This is in part because there is no way around sharing sensitive information in finance. In fact, there have been many major class action lawsuits due to compromised data within this vertical. Notably in 2019, Capital One Financial Corporation suffered a major breach that resulted in $80 million in fines, $190 million in paid settlements, and serious reputational damage.

Consumers are sensitive about their financial information. They demand assurance that the financial institution is collecting data responsibly, in a way that will not put them at risk. From a business standpoint, it's paramount that you ensure adherence to local privacy regulations and best practices, with an emphasis on ownership of first-party data. In this next section, we'll give you an overview of the industry at this time, some of the challenges it faces, privacy-centric solutions to employ, and smart next steps moving forward.

FINANCE IN THE NEW PRIVACY-CENTRIC REALITY

Consider the relationship most financial institutions share with their consumers. It's fundamentally predicated on trust. Most people are confident sharing their data with their banks and insurance providers, which suggests that the relationship is healthy. Considering this, winning in this industry isn't necessarily about developing better relationships (though that is always beneficial). Instead, it's about leveraging built-in advantages and expanding capability.

One such advantage is access to an incredibly large pool of first-party data, like bank statements, financial documents, transaction data, and tons of other information. This includes all the information from banking apps and websites. Of course, any time you see cross-channel data, user identifiers are necessary for cross-device analysis, channel analysis, and one-to-one user matching across different platforms.

According to Boston Consulting Group research, best-in-class advertisers can improve their technical data capabilities by adopting centralized data warehouses. There is a big focus on integrating multiple data sources to develop your own customized proprietary measurement algorithms in-house. These are just a handful of the considerations financial institutions need to make to update their privacy strategy.

This isn't to say that finance isn't ahead of the curve in some respects. While conducting strategic privacy risk assessments for various finance industry clients, we've witnessed that they've already embraced the cookieless future while many organizations are still gearing up for these technology changes to massively impact them. Yet people in the finance industry don't necessarily fully grasp that they're ahead of the curve because most of the news they see is more widely focused on the general market, whereas it's accelerated within their sector. Part of the challenge for finance is to recognize areas where they excel and areas with room for improvement.

Challenge: Fragmented User Experiences

One issue many finance industry organizations have is a very fragmented user experience, with various micro-applications and different websites. Yet many of them are not focused on consumer experience across those various platforms. Simply put, financial institutions need to pass "the grandma test," or the aforementioned test designed by our friend for her grandmother to ensure better user experience.

For example, American Express offered great rates for a savings account for their credit card customers. But once customers opened that account, they were prompted to create a new email and password. This was annoying on the consumer side, but potentially problematic for AmEx, too. Presumably, they couldn't stitch the data together on the back end, which meant that for consumers with both a credit card and a savings account, they had two data sets. They must have recognized the issue, as they now allow users to link their credit card and savings accounts together.

Solution: Unified Logins

Centralized logins present a massive opportunity to drive insights. If you have a central login portal, you also have that persistent identifier for a user across all of those different experiences. You can tie together that data set to learn even more about your customers.

In stark contrast to the AmEx example above, shoppers can easily navigate between Gap, Old Navy, and Banana Republic from the same website. They even share a checkout. From the user perspective, this means a great experience. It's easy to navigate between stores and returns are simple. From an organizational perspective, it means that the parent corporation can build incredibly rich consumer profiles effectively and easily.

Challenge: Accessing and Assessing First-Party Data

Despite a wealth of data, finance is also one of the industries most heavily regulated and prone to roadblocks to activate it. Personalization is limited directly in platforms like Google Ads for financial services such as home, car, and appliance loans; credit cards; and real estate to reduce societal biases. Google doesn't allow zip code, marital status, gender- or age-based targeting for a number of financial services. And crypto is even more heavily restricted.

Finance's biggest challenge is often how to better understand a user behavior segment so that they can personalize the experience without violating the trust relationship that they have with their consumers. Banking is strictly limited in terms of how much precision advertising can be legally conducted, as well as what is supported by the ad tech vendors.

That's a big divergence from other industries. A direct-to-consumer e-commerce company usually thinks about data in terms of audience creation and targeting. For finance, the question is how to safely collect information to create a better user experience, provide more personalized products, develop a deeper relationship, tie into the organization and brand, sell more products, and retain customers.

Solution: Better Value Propositions

Nearly every bank offers new customers a free checking account. And if you continue to browse, some may even incentivize you with a free $250. Clearly, financial institutions offer these incentives to attract new clients, but they also help to collect valuable first-party data. Based on the generous incentives, it's clear there is a lot of competition for customer data, and there isn't much space in the industry to increase financial incentives. One way that your institution can compete is by coming up with creative solutions to sweeten the deal.

Financial institutions aren't generally known for creative user experiences; most people don't comment on how much they love to use their bank's website or app. However, this trend is starting to change. With greater frequency, financial institutions are learning how to incentivize their users to engage on their platforms. Both large and local banks are realizing that an intuitive interface is a big selling point for their customers. Meanwhile, companies like Venmo have created social banking with an interactive platform where users are encouraged to share their transactions. Many investment companies have built clever apps that gamify saving and investing.

Not all financial institutions need to get terribly creative to obtain more first-party data. A study found that 69 percent of consumers would share significant data on their health, fitness, and driving habits in exchange for lower prices from insurers.[23] And as we alluded to earlier, there is a lot of room in the insurance space to increase engagement through clever apps and better user experience.

Challenge: Compliant Digital Marketing

A financial institution's ability to use digital marketing to grow relationships with consumers has always been one of the more challenging areas, even before new regulations. That's why many banks and credit card companies still use traditional strategies like cold calling and postcards. A lot of financial institutions are famous for giving away free checking accounts or even monetary incentives for opening a free checking account, which is another example of a more old-school approach to incentives.

The problem here is twofold: financial institutions can't use first-party data in the same way that other organizations do, which leads to incentive programs that can negatively impact the bottom line.

23 Kenneth Saldanha and Todd Staehle, "Guide Insurance Customers to Safety and Well-Being," Accenture, January 20, 2021, https://www.accenture.com/us-en/insights/insurance/guide-insurance-customers-safety-well-being.

Solution: Consent Management and Diverse Data Collection

Industries across the board must focus on integrating cookie consent management into their strategy, but it's even more critical for financial institutions to do so. In finance, there are usually many paths to purchase.

Diversify data collection to reduce risk and provide a more complete view of the user journey.

Challenge: Integration of All First-Party Data

Fragmented user journeys with multiple subdomains and logins increase complexity when integrating multiple data sources. For example, an insurance company may have a separate site for life insurance and another for car insurance.

Integration of all first-party data sources ensures advanced analytics capabilities. Offline conversion tracking is a strategy financial services can employ to achieve this goal. This method allows financial institutions to import conversions tracked in other systems into platforms like Google Ads. Examples include branch location data for customers applying for a mortgage or new account or calling into call centers for insurance quotes. Those interactions can be online, over the phone, or in person, making the combination of that data particularly useful.

One of the best use cases for integrated data is customer lifetime value modeling. While this model does take an initial investment of time and resources, it also provides a long-term solution to reach and convert the right customers to improve ROAS.

Solution: Segmentation

Segmentation is another area where the finance industry, banking or otherwise, has a natural built-in structure that they can leverage right away. Don't get bogged down in individual user journeys or insights for individuals. Find trends and general signals, focusing on segmentation. Segmenting or organizing users into common buckets allows you to develop experiences or activate strategies tailored to that group's behavior.

Different products often lend themselves to segmentation because of the product or account type that a person is using. In finance, customers are naturally segmenting themselves or the organization is segmenting users based on characteristics like how much money they have or what types of products they're interested in. For example, someone that has investment, checking, and savings accounts has a very different profile than someone with only a checking account. In this way, we lean on that segmentation to derive insights and then deliver customized experiences for each user perspective.

NEXT STEPS IN FINANCE

Building privacy-centric data capabilities in-house begins with the right team. More and more we see financial institutions employ a chief data officer with a number of data stakeholders with varying responsibilities nested under that position. There are still some siloed structures with owners and users of various data types like web analytics, marketing, CRM, IT, and compliance. Facilitating a cross-departmental privacy platform is a logical first step.

Even though data protection is nothing new in this industry, data protection officers (DPOs) and data privacy roles for media and marketing data are a slightly new concept. To be clear, there's always been data protection and security around general account data. But for media, the concept is somewhat new. And for finance specifically, it's important to lean on DPOs to define standards and paint a clear picture of the guardrails. Just because you have someone's information after they create an account with you does not mean you can use that information to target them.

In the near future, gain familiarity with the data your institution collects and what business purpose it serves. If there is no real business purpose or benefit, follow the principle of data minimization to reduce risk by eliminating the collection of unnecessary data.

A compliance audit is another important consideration. Ensure legal has the opportunity to speak with marketing stakeholders. The entire team needs to understand what the local policy changes are and how they impact the institution. Data owners should be aware of the data their team is responsible for and be vigilant in monitoring compliant data collection.

Finally, consider what to look for in a privacy consultant. Look for a privacy-centric partner that is forward thinking. They also must be familiar with the current trends and legal landscape unique to finance.

HEALTHCARE

CONTRIBUTOR HIGHLIGHT: JAMES LOVE

James is the Industry Team Lead for InfoTrust's healthcare and fitness digital analytics team. He's been at InfoTrust for over ten years, starting as a marketing intern out of the University of Cincinnati. Other previous roles include the Advertising Manager prior to InfoTrust's transition to a privacy-centric analytics solutions organization emphasizing measurement and optimization. In addition to leading an industry team of rock star analysts, James works with some of the largest organizations in the world, helping them advance their digital analytics maturity in a forward-thinking and strategic manner.

Outside of work, James enjoys attending Cincinnati Bearcats football and basketball games, and spending quality time with his beautiful wife and dogs.

In 2020, a Portuguese hospital was fined €400,000 for three GDPR violations.[24] This violation reveals that, despite healthcare's familiarity with regulations, new expectations are proving challenging for institutions to incorporate.

Because of new regulatory statutes, most healthcare information will fall under the category of sensitive data moving forward. That's true for all global regulations; there are significant limitations on how you can use medical data for advertising or targeting. In this next section, we'll provide an overview of the

24 Ana Menezes Monteiro, "First GDPR Fine in Portugal Issued against Hospital for Three Violations," International Association of Privacy Professionals, January 3, 2019, https://iapp.org/news/a/first-gdpr-fine-in-portugal-issued-against-hospital-for-three-violations/.

current state of healthcare, some of the privacy-centric solutions to employ, and smart next steps moving forward.

Healthcare in the New Privacy-Centric Reality

Perhaps more so than any other vertical, healthcare must emphasize ownership of first-party data. Further, server-side data distribution must be heavily prioritized by organizations in this particular industry due to the first-party control and security benefits that it can provide.

There are strict limitations regarding collection to consider. It takes explicit consent—even in the United States—to collect any health information. This includes explicit disclosure for exactly what that information is being used for, if you are processing that information, or whether you're using it for automated profiling.

Further, location data is now considered sensitive data. Even customer segmentation for personalization of a user's online experience will take explicit consent. This means use of data must be transparent and protected.

Consider the implications for strategic testing. Many optimization approaches in healthcare are reliant on methods like geolocation tests, which involve testing different strategies in specific locations to users within those parameters, and then measuring the incrementality of conversions that happen as a result of those changes. Much of the data you collect will not be available for precision advertising, to inform targeting, or any media optimization. Put simply: the challenge is not an inability to collect data, but to target the activities to a specific location with the inability to geo-locate.

Healthcare companies need to focus on the larger aggregate and on information that is freely given to them to perform any personalization activity. And yet, healthcare is no stranger to privacy rules because there have always been limitations on what information can be collected, shared, and used. Due to well-known regulations like HIPAA, security and protection are two mainstays of the industry.

Healthcare is continuing to digitize and is seeing an increase in the volume of patient interactions through their digital platforms. Many organizations now have an app, and most are seeing an increase in the volume of patient interactions on those apps. Digitization is mostly a positive trend. It reduces business costs and waste and catches up to the latest trends in customer service.

But again, some issues holding the industry back from speeding up the process of digitization are stringent privacy data regulations, including HIPAA and other protected health information (PHI). Healthcare organizations must create relevant, personalized, and timely communications tailored to individual preferences, as well as ensuring that high-risk individuals receive the follow-ups they need. At the end of the day, healthcare needs to remove friction in their interactions with consumers/patients.

Challenge: Using First-Party Data

Healthcare providers have access to unique first-party data sets. From payment information to demographics to sensitive health information, this industry knows a lot about its patients. However, that doesn't mean that first-party data can be used in whatever way you wish. Most of this data shouldn't be used for advertising. For example, it's poor practice to target people based on the type of surgery they have or advertise a specific drug for a condition that you wouldn't otherwise know about without access to PHI.

Solution: Clever Use of Contextual Data

Without being able to use much of the vast first-party data collected, the healthcare industry must get creative. One of our clients uses predictive weather forecasting to promote drugs that are often taken when the weather starts to get colder. A consumer can click on an ad on a weather site, go to the web page, and input their email in return for a coupon. Because of the method of collection, the client can now use that first-party data with fewer restrictions.

Clearly, there is a very thin line to walk when targeting patients. There is a lot for your team to consider with respect to compliance in healthcare. This is an industry where the legal and compliance team should be deeply involved in marketing and targeting. Ensure your organization is aware of all regulations every step of the way.

Challenge: Cost to Attract New Patients

Another challenge facing healthcare is the cost to attract a new patient. Research suggests it is much less expensive to retain patients than to acquire new ones. According to Adrienne Boissy, Chief Customer Experience Officer at the Cleveland Clinic, it costs seven times more to bring a lapsed patient back into their health system than to retain and build upon existing patient relationships.[25] With this in mind, organizations need

---

25 "GoLIVE Webinar: Elevating Care for Patients while Reducing Stress for Clinicians," HLTH, video, 1:21:03, January 8, 2021, https://www.youtube.com/watch?v=LqbGGUYQOo8.

to incorporate and prioritize smart strategies to retain patients long term.

Solution: Better User Experience

A great experience at a dental office isn't just a good cleaning. It's the ability to receive an appointment reminder on your phone and an event in your calendar. And to not have to deal with those handwritten cards or be asked for an email address again and again. Once friction is removed, attracting new patients through referrals is a bit more straightforward.

NEXT STEPS FOR HEALTHCARE

Because healthcare is such a highly regulated industry, the concept of data minimization is particularly relevant. It's imperative that organizations limit the collection of personal information to cases where it's directly relevant and necessary to accomplish a specific goal. Healthcare organizations should prioritize A/B testing to optimize first-party data collection. If you ask for a phone number, does it decrease conversion? Is it worth it to collect that number, knowing that users are more likely to read an email from their provider? A logical first step for any healthcare organization is putting data minimization practices in place.

Moving forward, organizations should consider how they can prioritize follow-up with patients. In particular, high-risk individuals should receive notifications of upcoming appointments. Tools that pass the "grandma test" (like mobile apps and websites) and remove friction should be at top of mind to help retain patients and ensure they get the care they deserve.

Team composition in healthcare in the privacy-centric future should include internal IT and tag management teams due to the risk of publishing a non-compliant tag. Build a team of forward-thinking analysts and marketers, but don't stop there. It's imperative to break down the interdepartmental silos between IT and marketing.

When looking for a privacy partner, healthcare organizations should prioritize one that is privacy-centric, forward thinking, and focused on first-party data. The truth is that many healthcare organizations aren't as proactive in developing an innovative data strategy as they should be. If you still rely on third-party data, you are not only leaving your organization vulnerable, but you aren't investing in a foundation for the future.

CONSUMER PACKAGED GOODS

CONTRIBUTOR HIGHLIGHT: TOM LUNDIN

Tom is the Industry Team Lead for InfoTrust's consumer packaged goods and multi-brand team. Working with a team of talented analysts from five countries and three continents, the group leads the digital analytics strategy and implementations for some of the world's largest organizations. He has over fifteen years of experience in the digital analytics industry and enjoys the daily challenge of adapting the ever-changing landscape of digital analytics tools to each company's unique organizational structure and needs, all with an eye to the critical importance of privacy and global consumer data regulations.

When away from his desk, you'll usually find Tom outside with his family, exploring the natural beauty that Pennsylvania has to offer on a bike ride, paddling down a stream, or hiking through the woods.

Due to the scale of consumer packaged goods (CPG) companies, these organizations are understandably concerned about regulatory challenges. There are so many requirements across so many markets, you can't have a one-size-fits-all strategy, yet you also can't have an "every single country has its own rules" approach. It's just not operationally feasible. Finding that middle ground of defining global standards, integrating some customization for regional standards, and then allowing for a little bit of personalization at individual country and market levels is critical for regulatory adherence. In this next section, we'll provide an overview of the current state of CPGs, the challenges they face, solutions they can deploy, and next steps moving forward.

CPG IN THE NEW PRIVACY-CENTRIC REALITY

Consumer packaged goods (CPG), or multi-brand product manufacturers, often have a less-direct digital touchpoint with their consumers. As such, many organizations are heavily reliant on third-party data. But they are also less informed about the ongoing shift away from third-party cookies. This leaves them particularly vulnerable in the new privacy-centric reality.

One of our large CPG clients is near the top ten companies in global advertising spend. After an internal analysis, they learned that 80 percent of their media spend was targeted against third-party cookies.

There are two major concerns for CPG moving forward. The first is first-party data collection. Organizations want to know how they can collect first-party data in a compliant and transparent way across a shifting international framework of privacy legislation. Considering that most CPGs are global companies, the patchwork nature of privacy regulations is especially challenging.

Second, CPGs wonder how they can empower their brands to effectively reach consumers while still protecting the organization (and the consumers) from badly planned and implemented tracking practices. Continuity is always a challenge for CPG, and this is especially true considering new regulations.

Challenge: Executive Turnover

We've advised many CMOs and other executives in the CPG vertical over the last decade. In that time, they've moved between three or even four companies. This turnover can often be attributed to their success. They'll enter an organization, orchestrate a transformation, and then look to the next company to deliver the same results.

Whenever we bring on a new client who has just moved into a new organization, their first question to us is what to keep and what to toss within their data privacy and overall marketing strategy and stack. Those who we personally advise will deliver consistent standards across organizations. But what about the people who replace them?

Without a strong foundation, it's often easier for new leadership to start from scratch, rather than revive an unclear but existing policy. The problem then becomes the organization has a new strategy every two to four years, starting from ground zero every time. That is not a sustainable model, especially as privacy expectations continue to grow.

Solution: Adoptable Privacy Strategy

Whether it be the executive leadership or a privacy partner, someone needs to first put in place a strong privacy strategy to build a foundation. From there, leadership or an outside partner needs to introduce the privacy strategy to any new decision-maker within the organization.

Keep in mind, when scaling solutions to hundreds or thousands of websites, you'll need to decide how much customization will be allowed for your markets and brands. Do you support a single consent configuration globally? Or do you support two, five, or fifty? The added granularity in allowed consent configurations can provide flexibility but can also significantly increase complexity of deployment, governance, and monitoring.

Increased complexity means additional costs in implementing and maintaining those platforms and also translates to greater risk of non-compliance through mistakes in configuration or markets that don't adapt to future changes in legislation. Further, the more complex, the less transferrable the strategy.

Challenge: Lack of Direct Consumer Relationships

CPGs face an interesting challenge: they do not have direct consumer relationships. A consumer may buy a product from a brand, but they are interacting with a sales or retail partner to do so. This means that CPG companies themselves do not have macro conversion or transaction information. However, they can acquire that information from retail partners (second-party data), although we expect challenges around data sharing will only increase in the future.

With third-party cookies going away and cross-site, cross-device identifiers being shielded or fully deprecated, it's difficult or near impossible to link data sets together across different digital assets. Lack of visibility due to that natural structure is a huge challenge.

There are also fewer opportunities for first-party data collection through registrations and brand-owned websites. If you want to buy dish soap, you may be more inclined to go to Amazon or Walmart versus P&G's brand website. There are so few opportunities to get any one-to-one persistent user-given identifiers or user-provided information in this space.

Solution #1: Creative Ways to Acquire First-Party Data

For CPG industries to address that challenge of lack of direct access to identifiers, they need to focus on more creative solutions for registration and logins and creative solutions for those one-to-one interactions directly between the brand and the consumer.

Remember when there used to be crossword puzzles or other games printed on cereal boxes? One of our large CPG clients has built augmented reality campaigns that bring back that experience. A QR code on the box allows someone to have a unique experience, whether it's a game, health tips, or a history lesson. This is just one creative example of how CPGs can bring customers into their ecosystem.

Finesse is critical in creative strategies. The result is often clunky when CPGs try to pull off tech-heavy campaigns themselves. These initiatives have to be fun and intuitive for the user. And of course, they must actually be helpful for the organization.

Solution #2: Leverage Second-Party Data

As we move away from third-party data, new ways of modeling to fill gaps in first-party data become even more important. For any modeling and machine learning to take place, we need input data. There are minimum threshold amounts and minimum volumes of data necessary to train those models to give accurate information and meaningful insights.

CPG organizations often need to rely on channel partners to generate insights to use for optimization. Due to the purchasing of consumer goods happening via retail partners, CPGs often will know who their customers are (via direct digital relationships, loyalty programs, and so on) but have no way of understanding buying behavior with their own first-party data sets. New technologies like clean rooms enable the aggregation of consumer information (first-party owned by the CPG) and shopper behavior (second-party owned by the retail partner). Modeling and doing advanced analysis with this data set allows CPGs to better attribute conversions with media activities, understand consumer time to reorder, and identify complementary products to leverage in campaign content.

NEXT STEPS FOR CPG ORGANIZATIONS

The first step for CPG organizations is to recognize that the global patchwork of ever-changing privacy regulations will complicate their strategy. The best approach is to ensure that all tracking is done with transparent, honest, and privacy-centric data collection practices. Next, you can thoughtfully build out necessary additions and customizations to allow markets to adapt the flexible, privacy-first model to the specific requirements of their country or region.

Effective team composition in CPG relies on collaboration. Typically, legal teams should be involved in most conversations around what data can be collected in each market. Ad-tech teams can then help define what data is necessary to collect for marketing success in their brands. Next, development teams can help implement and manage the collection.

CPGs are often decentralized and give a high degree of autonomy to brands and markets around the world. This makes them nimble in their region, but also makes building in-house capabilities a challenge. Rather than directly supporting implementations, organizations should focus in-house capabilities on setting and defining global data collection standards as well as communicating and training individual markets and brands to implement and follow those standards.

Having a champion for these initiatives in each market is critical to success given the decentralized nature of most CPG organizations. The champions can translate the needs of the brands in the market, work within the framework of their local privacy legislation, and monitor the ongoing adherence and compliance of their data collection.

When choosing a privacy partner, look for a team with a proven track record in CPG with the experience and privacy know-how to guide you through the ever-changing privacy landscape. They'll need familiarity and advanced experience with scalable automation solutions to deploy changes to hundreds or thousands of GA or GTM assets at a time.

DIRECT-TO-CONSUMER (D2C) E-COMMERCE AND RETAIL

CONTRIBUTOR HIGHLIGHT: KRISTI MORIN

Kristi is an Industry Team Lead for InfoTrust's Direct-to-Consumer digital analytics team. She has been a consultant in the marketing analytics field for over fifteen years with experience spanning multiple vertices including online, print, B2B, and DTRV. Her career fulfillment comes from helping to support her retail clients that have digital storefronts to plan and execute strong analytic strategies that become foundational to informing their general business and marketing optimization decision-making.

Outside of InfoTrust, Kristi is a proud mom of two beautiful little girls. And because two kids aren't enough to keep her busy on the weekends, she is also the founder and President of a local 501(c)(3) nonprofit organization that organizes social activities for other working moms in her local area to meet and mingle with each other. If she ever does opt for a career change, it will definitely be to pursue her passion for event planning!

CONTRIBUTOR HIGHLIGHT: COURTNEY FENSTERMAKER

Courtney is an Industry Team Lead for InfoTrust's Direct-to-Consumer digital analytics team. Starting her career in digital marketing consulting, she brings a strategic, "big-picture" perspective of how our clients can best leverage their data for marketing activation and insight generation. Since then, Courtney has focused her career on first-party data strategies and privacy-centric digital analytics practices to help retail and e-commerce organizations build a genuine and trusting connection with their customers.

Outside of InfoTrust, Courtney is also passionate about her involvement in the Digital Analytics Association (DAA), where she sits in key roles on the Privacy and Ethics Committee and the Implementation Task Force, and acts as a Women in Analytics (WIA) mentor. In her free time, she loves attending a game at her local AAA baseball stadium or checking out the newest restaurants in the area with her husband.

Direct-to-consumer (D2C) industries have an incredible advantage in the new privacy-centric reality. Their secret weapon? Direct consumer relationships. They manage the actual purchasing process, which means they have full interaction with the consumer across the entire funnel. D2C's biggest advantage is also its greatest challenge. All that information across platforms makes it critical for leaders of D2C companies to integrate online and offline across activation platforms.

Perhaps no other industry is as impacted by the deprecation of third-party cookies as D2C. New regulations impact conversion tracking, view-through and multi-touch attribution, audience targeting, and frequency capping. With the shift toward a cookieless experience, D2C brands will need to explore new ways to target users without the use of pseudonymous identifiers. This next section will offer an overview of D2C, some of the challenges it faces, solutions to deploy, and smart next steps.

D2C IN THE NEW PRIVACY-CENTRIC REALITY

Data segmentation is key for D2C organizations. The first type of data to discuss is named addressable user data, which is any consenting user with an identifier or users that have registered and logged in. Organizations can leverage technologies like a CDP to manage all of that user data in-house. Once you have standardization, you can start unifying CRM data or data from offline sales channel partners with the digital CDP data.

Internal analysis across e-commerce D2C organizations revealed that about 6 percent of online users fall into that named user category, meaning that the brand has a persistent identifier and a direct relationship with that customer. That 6 percent account for over 40 percent of digital transactions and revenue. Even without a fancy CLV analysis, we can see that this is a very valuable cohort!

Named and addressable users create a very valuable cohort. Not only are they a lucrative group, but they also offer incredible insight. Because they are trackable, they offer visibility into their entire journey, including their interactions with your brands across domains. But that's not all. You can also find common characteristics, and then use those characteristics to match to your wider user base so that you can then segment and target accordingly. The other type of data that is especially relevant to D2C organizations is anonymous interaction and campaign data. By reviewing these data sets, you can gain insights into customer behavior across various locations by performing aggregate trend analyses.

Once you understand what needs to be collected, standardization of those data structures and taxonomies becomes critical in the D2C vertical due to the volume of partners that these companies work with. A CPG organization might have 85 to 90 percent of their spend just with Google because they focus on search and branding campaigns. Typical e-commerce D2C organizations split that spend among Google, Facebook, Twitter, TikTok, and other programmatic partners. They also work with distributors like Amazon. All this to say that standardization is paramount to enable integration and drive cross channel insights.

Further, D2C organizations must prioritize migration to server-side data distribution. By doing so, they can send data to an owned first-party data warehouse for advanced analysis and modeling. Keep in mind, D2C's biggest asset is their ability to mine massive data sets for signals. The key is having everything structured in such a way that you're actually able to lean on it and leverage it, which is the biggest challenge that many organizations come to us with.

D2C companies must provide a value-add to customers for providing their data in an effort to tie in offline and online experience. A common but sometimes poor incentive is rewards programs and discounts. This strategy works great for some brands but can devalue others. Creative companies look to other incentives that don't dramatically impact their bottom line, like the ability to store orders for easy returns or a more seamless site experience.

Data exchange will always be required for certain purchases and online retail participation, but how that data is handled and protected, and how user requests are responded to, is what will separate the trustworthy companies from those that lose the consumer expectation battle. Be transparent and work alongside users to share what data has been accumulated and how you are protecting their data.

Challenge: Balancing Personalization and Privacy

Consumers want both personalization and privacy, which can be challenging to deliver simultaneously. Someone may want a company to remember their payment preferences at checkout, for example, but they might not want them to give their email to their other stores. Someone may want a site to remember their shoe size, but not their credit card number.

In this way, customers have a love-hate relationship with personalization. They expect and dislike it at the same time. Research shows that 76 percent of customers expect a personalized experience. Simultaneously, over-personalized experience can feel like an intrusion, and 52 percent of shoppers already worry about retailers knowing too much.

Solution: Testing

The solution is a balanced approach. Customize customer content and offers while being subtle rather than pushy. But how do you walk that fine line? Test, test, and retest. Implement changes slowly and thoughtfully.

For example, if a D2C clothing store currently does not filter sizes based on the user profile, they could begin testing how users respond to that kind of personalization. If they deselect the option, then you understand that they did not prefer that kind of personalization. In this way, organizations can slowly pilot new personalization initiatives and build trust.

Challenge: Data Protection

Storing data brings risks in the form of cyberattacks. Failure to protect and respect customer data can subject companies to regulatory penalties, lawsuits, as well as loss of business associated with their site being deemed "unsafe." Once a company loses a consumer's trust with something as precious to them as their financial data, it's unlikely the consumer will ever purchase from them again. For this reason, brand equity makes data protection particularly important in the D2C vertical.

Solution: Better Data Security

Data security comes in two forms: invisible and visible. Let's start with invisible security.

To provide invisible security, regularly audit tracking tags, understand what data is being collected, and where it is being collected from. Next, apply cybersecurity and encrypt sensitive data by putting it behind a firewall.

Another way to increase invisible security is to isolate sensitive data from personal data. Using data buckets will ensure that the proper protection is in place based on the kind of data collected. Lastly, ensure you educate all employees, even remote and freelance, on security risks. When it comes to data privacy and protection, any siloed departments are a liability.

Visible security comes in the form of transparency. Document and communicate privacy initiatives to customers clearly in a straightforward way. Leverage visuals and graphics that make the customer feel safe shopping. Some examples include safe payment icons and customer testimonials.

It's important to understand that not all data is breached from external sources. This means it's a good idea to ensure a digital audit and log system is implemented. One way to ensure data safety is to employ a customer data platform (CDP). CDPs are privacy-friendly solutions to collect first-party data from various sources and use to intelligently market to customers and maximize their value.

Challenge: Gaining Insight from First-Party Data

D2C organizations have a lot of access to first-party data. But that doesn't mean they are leveraging the biggest source of first-party data effectively. Many D2C organizations don't ask their loyal customers enough questions or use the data they offer up freely. If customers trust you, they often want to provide additional information about themselves, especially when incentivized.

Many D2C brands fail to gain insight because they do not properly segment their user groups. The truth is that you'll never design an experience that satisfies everyone. The question then becomes how you can segment your audience. You may be investing a lot to acquire first-party data. But without segmentation, are you activating on it? You could be missing a massive opportunity.

Solution: Segmentation

Segmenting your loyal customers is a key strategy to gain insight. Once segmented, you can gain better insights from them. For example, beauty brands can offer personalized products if customers input data like their skin type or preferred shade. Brands like Benjamin Moore or Macy's can ask about a customer's preferred style to upsell or personalize experience to certain styles. In this way, brands can do a better job of gaining insight from their most valuable customers.

Challenge: Disjointed User Data Sets

If you have multiple brands, are you able to track named and addressable users across sites? Can you unify what that consumer does both offline and online? Some stores actually change their loyalty program based on where the customer is buying and whether they buy in-store or offline. From a first-party data perspective, having multiple data sets for a single user is a losing strategy. Further, it makes compliance more complicated and deletion requests a nightmare.

Solution: Unify the Experience

D2C organizations need to unify the user experience. Create a single login for users across sites. Build loyalty programs that are accessible on- and offline to integrate interactions from the web and in-store. This will ensure that your data set remains robust for your most valued customers. Further, it means that compliance will be straightforward (as long as you are following the principles outlined in Chapter Five).

NEXT STEPS FOR D2C

D2C brands should continue to create genuine customer experiences based on personalization and improved user experience. To increase access to first-party data and increase customer lifetime value, brands should market to current customers in an effort to retain and create raving fans from their existing customer base.

Next, reevaluate your tech and marketing stacks. Consider how the tools at your disposal will change with the depreciation of third-party cookies.

Begin preparing for the transition now. Don't wait until

enforcement to get your privacy strategy in place or to get the right people in the right seats. Updating your privacy strategy requires a team effort that includes cross-organization alignment and support. This support should stem from leadership.

When evaluating a privacy partner, look for a team that puts privacy at the forefront of their work, not as an afterthought. Your partner should view privacy changes as an opportunity for growth, not as an inconvenience that needs to be worked around.

CROSS-INDUSTRY INSIGHTS

Each industry encounters unique challenges and must come up with novel solutions. If a problem arises and you do not see the solution in your own industry, look to see what others are doing. In the beginning of this chapter, we argued that organizations can set consumer expectations across industries.

Consumers now expect the same level of information safety in the D2C space that they expect from their financial institutions. They expect the kind of customization and automation they enjoy in the D2C vertical in healthcare. They want privacy, but also personalization. In this way, brands in the privacy-centric future must look across industries to adopt the best strategy. Don't be afraid to test strategies from your neighbors.

Now that you understand how your industry is currently impacted by a greater demand for privacy, it's time to look ahead. The next chapter reveals how you can build your future-proof strategy.

CHAPTER EIGHT

DESIGN YOUR FUTURE-PROOF ORGANIZATION

You already have a five-step plan (provided in Chapter 4) to adopt a privacy-centric strategy. But once that is in place, what then? We've given you the tools and knowledge to build a strategy for the privacy-centric future. We've shown you what to do internally and what to look for in a partner. We've told you how to collect and store data, and even given you industry-specific advice.

But our work wouldn't be complete without looking even further ahead.

As organizations look to the future, much remains unknown. But what we can say for certain is that the brands that will thrive are the ones that are willing to experiment. Over 1,300 experiments from Google to Amazon to Netflix show that time and time again, organizations that experiment are the ones that come out on top. But we aren't advocating you experiment for experimentation's sake. Experimentation allows you to learn more about new technologies and capabilities. And more about your consumers and their preferences. And as you learn and collect data, you give yourself permission to be more decisive.

In an article on leadership, the *Harvard Business Review* argued that decisiveness is the key to success, writing "High-performing CEOs do not necessarily stand out for making great decisions all the time; rather, they stand out for being more decisive. They make decisions earlier, faster, and with greater conviction."[26] You don't need to be a CEO to derive insight from the quote—it applies to anyone in a position to make decisions. And to make good decisions, you need information.

To get that information, you must continuously stage experiments.

BECOME A CULTURE OF EXPERIMENTATION

The more experiments you conduct, the more robust your data set. We encourage you to try server-side tag management and other data collection and storage strategies. We hope you test for better user experience. And we urge you to properly segment your data. We also hope you experiment for a better value proposition.

We aren't talking about tweaking your newsletter sign-up or the color of your website. We're talking about thinking outside the box to deliver a user experience where your customers actually want to give you their personal data because what they receive in return is so valuable to them.

---

26 Elena Lytkina Botelho et al., "What Sets Successful CEOs Apart," *Harvard Business Review*, May–June 2017, https://hbr.org/2017/05/what-sets-successful-ceos-apart.

When you visit Walt Disney World, you are given a wristband. This wristband optimizes your experience, allowing you to purchase admittance to a shorter line, pay at restaurants, and access other benefits. In exchange, the wristband allows Disney to collect data for all of these interactions. This data enables them to optimize pricing, promotions, experience design, and marketing. End to end, this experiment initially cost the company around $1 billion. Disney was willing to make big bets on data solutions that dramatically improved user experience. And they felt comfortable doing so because they had the data to back up the investment.

Once you have the data, you will be able to continuously test to build a better value proposition. Test to own your data. Define your own structure. Hire partners to give outside perspectives. Create holistic, multi-orchestration changes that propel you into the future.

Exponential experimentation is the best way to prepare your organization for what's coming next.

LOOK TO THE FUTURE: WEB3

The internet as we know it today is a highly interactive place, which has driven the digital marketing industry to become the hyper-targeted environment we're currently familiar with. But this wasn't always the case.

The first version of the web that became widespread was more informational than interactive. The pages you could visit were static, so the ads placed on them were contextual rather than targeted. For example, if you visited the website of a sporting goods store, the ads would include things like sports gear, team merchandise, and sporting events. We can think of this as Web1. Ad placement in Web1 was based on the context of where it would be seen, with an understanding of the interests likely held by the people visiting a specific site.

While it's no longer common for digital marketing in most industries, we do still see contextual advertising today, mainly in the news media. Even as news outlets have shifted from print to broadcast to digital, the ads they run are largely based on the context of the content they publish. For example, a news site running an article on a local marathon event held every year might include an ad for a retailer that sells athletic shoes on that article's page. The news media never really left the contextual advertising model because its user base is mainly local people clicking on different articles—but the content is by nature more specific, and therefore easier to tailor ads to the interests of the people consuming that content.

Around 2004 we entered Web2, in which the dynamic shifted with the addition of interactive elements that birthed social media and e-commerce. This led to the boom of marketing technology because rich user information was so easy and cheap to collect, and there was no concept of consent around data collection. Advertising became largely dependent on tracking users across the internet. The more robust the user profile, the better the ROI.

Around 2016, the concept of user privacy and legality entered the space. Now Web3 is forming before our eyes, and it's a place where we must consider the societal expectations of data collection and user preference. Web3 uses blockchain technology to change how information is stored, shared, and owned.

Due to the disruptive potential of blockchain, advocates argue that Web3 will create digital economies, new kinds of products, and novel online services. Some even claim that it will return democracy to the web. One thing is certain: Web3 will define the next era of the internet.

The transition between Web2 and Web3 is an incredible moment in history. Of particular interest to marketers is the movement from a centralized web to a decentralized one. Centralized internet networks employ single servers that manage all data processing. That means all the data is funneled through a single point, where it can then be used for whatever purpose the organization controlling the server has. Historically, centralization has helped some organizations produce mind-boggling wealth for themselves and their shareholders by hoovering up users' data and selling targeted ads against it. As it turns out, all those free services weren't actually free at all. Users just didn't understand the implications of that bargain.

Comparing Web Versions

	Web 1.0 Basic Encyclopedias	Web 2.0 Social Networks	Web 3.0 Assistants, Clouds
Content	Static, read-only content	Shared, dynamic content	Content-connection-based through search and analysis
Interaction	No interaction	User interaction	AI-driven services
Focus	Company-based	Community-based	Individual-based

© InfoTrust

Advocates of Web3 recognize the value of consumer data. The decentralized nature of the blockchain allows users to take back ownership of their data at a time when the general population is beginning to recognize that their personal information has incredible value.

So what will this mean for *you*?

The short answer might annoy you: we don't know. Certainly this will impact organizations that have established themselves as privacy brands. But how it will impact the average business is hard to say. The only true way to find out is to experiment with Web3 technology.

MARKETING IN THE METAVERSE

Definitions of the metaverse vary, but they have a few commonalities. Most agree that the metaverse actually comprises many metaverses, or decentralized digital spaces. These spaces are considered augmented and virtual reality. Another key component of the metaverse is the use of blockchain. Each metaverse stores information on the blockchain and allows users to own digital goods.

The metaverse holds untapped potential for marketing. What if a buyer could enter your virtual store and try on virtual clothing? What if they could interact with your products up close, from their living room? Think about what the TV did for brands in the 1940s—we're talking about that same sort of seismic shift here. Suddenly, organizations could create whole shopping experiences for their buyers in their own homes. But in the metaverse, it's a two-way conversation, as buyers can interact with brands and products.

It is critical to rethink how we measure marketing success in the metaverse. Appropriate metrics may not be what we expect. How do you translate the number of visitors, conversions, "likes," and shares, as well as the cost of acquiring customers in a space with anonymity? With the metaverse, marketers may need to create new engagement metrics to define interactions with players.

NFTS, WALLETS, AND CONSUMER IDENTITY

Marketing in Web3 will take place in digital spaces like OM and Decentraland—virtual, 3D browser-based platforms. Inside, users can inhabit virtual plots of land, interact with other users, explore, shop, and have other virtual experiences.[27]

Customers who want to shop in these virtual spaces use a digital wallet. A digital wallet, such as MetaMask, allows the user to make electronic transactions with a second party using digital currency, like crypto.[28] Generally, users are buying NFTs. **Non-fungible tokens** (NFTs) are records of ownership stored on the blockchain. These records of ownership can be for digital assets or even real-world objects.

Unlike online content on Web2, NFTs have unique identifying codes and cannot be copied, substituted, or subdivided, which brings scarcity into the market. This means NFTs representing ownership of real-world items with a limited run, like flagship products or classic models, can be an interesting use case.

---

27 https://oncyber.io/6529om; https://decentraland.org/.

28 https://metamask.io/.

There are a few forward-thinking companies that are already experimenting in this space.

Acura, the luxury division of Honda, announced that the first 500 customers to reserve a 2023 Integra would also receive a 3D image of the car. Acura also built what they call the "first immersive auto showroom experience within the metaverse." It's called the Acura of Decentraland, and inside users can walk around 3D models of the cars and even try on Acura's clothing via their avatar.[29]

But marketing in this space doesn't have to stay in the metaverse. There is a lot of opportunity for hybrid products that transcend the virtual space. Experiments are currently happening with online-to-offline and other monetization models. While these experiments are often meant to attract the attention of difficult-to-reach user groups, build valuable brand communities, and drive action in the real world, a number of challenges persist.

One downside of selling digital products is their limited applicability outside of their platforms of origin. The lack of interoperability between Web3 platforms is an obstacle to greater customer adoption and to greater utility of brand-generated tokens and digital assets.

Another challenge is monetization of Web3 assets. Many marketers and consumers alike still consider artifacts like NFTs to be PR experiments when driven by brands.

---

29 "Acura Enters the Metaverse with Integra NFT and First-Ever Virtual Auto Showroom," news release, Acura, March 10, 2022, https://acuranews.com/en-US/releases/release-b7c602e7f6feb65d30b129b0f61a0e59-acura-enters-the-metaverse-with-integra-nft-and-first-ever-virtual-auto-showroom.

Near term, the biggest potential of digital products is in customer intelligence. Marketers can use digital assets, which are cheaper to produce than physical goods, to quickly gauge the appeal of a product aesthetic or design, and companies can then turn the most popular virtual items into physical ones.

USER INSIGHTS IN WEB3

We've discussed how Web3 creates greater anonymity, and how that will pose a challenge to marketers trying to build customer profiles. But even though crypto wallets make the user anonymous, the transactions on the blockchain are public. So when a consumer mints your flagship NFT, you can see every other transaction that's ever been associated with that specific wallet. Furthermore, the blockchain is immutable, meaning that nothing written to it can be deleted.

The potential of this for marketers is massive. Not only can you view all other assets your consumers have purchased, but also the amounts paid, frequency of purchases, and from where those purchases came. The potential for segmentation, insights, and understanding to inform marketing decisions in this environment is mind boggling.

On the other hand, this immutability of blockchain is possible to create a lot of headaches for global privacy regulators, considering the right to be forgotten and the right to request data deletion. Companies selling products to consumers that want to become early players in Web3 will have to keep this in mind. Just because you are marketing in a new environment doesn't mean the first rule of privacy-centricity—respecting the privacy rights of users—no longer applies.

A hybrid approach to the blockchain does exist. It's called self-sovereign identity (SSI). SSI is a process in which a user's ID credential is stored and managed by that user. To reach that information, other parties need their consent. The implications here are twofold. One, users can customize what information they want brands or anyone else to see. The second is that they could potentially sell access to this information. In this way, consumers are now the ones selling and profiting off their own data.

Brave browser is an example of a solution introducing a version of this. Brave is a free and open-source web browser that is privacy-focused. In addition to blocking online advertisements and trackers by default, users accessing the web with Brave are actually paid for their data on the blockchain. This happens through the distribution of their own cryptocurrency, Brave Attention Token, in exchange for the user viewing ads served through the browser. When we said that consumer data was going to get more expensive, we weren't kidding. Pay-to-play could be the not-too-distant future of digital marketing. But just how much influence will it have over your business?

THE REALITY OF WEB3

A lot of the consumers and many technologists are getting excited about the concept of cutting out the go-between through decentralization. New technologies introduced by Web3 like smart contracts and distributed transaction ledgers could reduce agency costs, eliminate billing discrepancies, and work a lot of inefficiencies out of the supply chain. That's the promise of decentralization—but does this match the reality?

If we're being honest, most people don't want or know how to run technologies necessary to interact with Web3 at this time. Few want to learn how to write code to buy a pair of shoes.

But that doesn't mean there isn't enormous potential in Web3. Blockchain technology, NFTs, and smart contracts do have the power to change the dynamic between consumer data and marketing efforts. And this period of disruption offers an incredible opportunity for businesses that are willing to experiment in the metaverse. Familiar brands like Gucci, P&G, Coca-Cola, Campbell Soup, and Patrón Tequila are just a few examples of organizations that are already exploring the metaverse.

And that is what is most important: experimentation. Just as you must experiment with new ways to gather first-party data, new models to mine insights from different user cohorts, and new strategies for reaching users on the privacy-centric web, you need to experiment in new digital spaces such as Web3. The future is unknown, but it is undoubtedly one that will value experimentation.

To prove that we practice what we preach, check out the QR code to the first-ever InfoTrust NFT at the beginning of the book. Will it increase our revenue? We don't know. But we do know that if we want to remain a company, we must be willing to navigate uncharted waters.

THE NEXT STEP

ACCESS YOUR FREE STRATEGIC RISK ASSESSMENT

As you begin building your new strategy, keep in mind the three pillars of privacy.

Principle One: Respect the Rights of Users

Principle Two: First-Party Ownership of First-Party Data

Principle Three: Action from Analysis and Insight

Pillars of Privacy-Centric Marketing

© InfoTrust

We built every strategy and insight in this book based on those three principles. If you adopt each, you'll build a strong privacy culture. But of course, strong doesn't necessarily mean that privacy is your winning aspiration. As we discussed, the true power of our strategy is in the ability to tailor it to the needs of your organization.

Whether you'll use privacy to gain a competitive edge or simply become compliant, refer to the 6 "P"s of digital analytics transformation. With your purpose, people, platforms, process, pace, and payoff clear, you can begin to define and execute your privacy-centric marketing transformation road map.

We understand that implementation can be difficult, especially when faced with looming government regulations and technological changes. To help our readers meet their goal faster, we are offering our readers a free, online risk assessment. It will help you evaluate the vulnerability of your organization using the following criteria:

- Quality of actionable first-party data
- Third-party cookie dependency
- Risks due to user opt-out
- Strategic risk based upon tactics used for advertising activation

To access your free risk assessment, follow the QR code below.

The future is privacy-centric. The organizations that understand what an equal value exchange looks like will be the ones best positioned to excel. Remember, to succeed in this new world, your approach to privacy must be predicated on respect. And if you follow the path we've outlined in this book, you'll unlock the power of a privacy-centric organization.

Prepare to run.

AUTHORS AND CONTRIBUTORS

LUCAS LONG

Lucas Long is Director of Privacy Strategy at InfoTrust, working with global organizations at the intersection of digital strategy, privacy regulations, and technical data collection architecture. Through these efforts, he helps companies understand their limitations for data enablement due to privacy challenges and design optimal ways to accomplish core use cases in a compliant manner. When not discussing the intricacies of GDPR and cookie laws with clients, Lucas enjoys traveling and exploring new cultures, one bite at a time. Based in Barcelona, he is also a presenter and contributing writer, featured at industry events organized by Google, the Digital Analytics Association, and the *Journal of Applied Marketing Analytics.*

ALEX YASTREBENETSKY

Alex Yastrebenetsky is CEO and co-founder of InfoTrust, a privacy-centric digital analytics solutions company. Under his leadership, InfoTrust has received numerous awards, including being named to the following lists: *Fortune* Best Small & Medium Workplaces, Ad Age Best Places to Work, Inc. 5000, and Inc. Best Workplaces. Outside of work, Alex is very passionate about supporting the local community, especially education and children's health causes. In 2020, Alex was an EY Entrepreneur of the Year Finalist for the East Central Region.

Alex is the author of Amazon #1 bestseller *Crawl, Walk, Run.*

MICHAEL LOBAN

Michael Loban is the Chief Growth Officer at InfoTrust, a global privacy-centric digital analytics solutions company. He is also coauthor of the Amazon bestselling book *Crawl, Walk, Run: Advancing Analytics Maturity with Google Marketing Platform.* When he is not motivating organizations to undertake a digital transformation, Michael can be found passing on the power of digital analytics to the next generation of marketers and analysts as a member of the Xavier University Williams College of Business Executive Advisory board and Term Adjunct Professor at the University of Cincinnati. He is also a presenter and contributing writer, with work published in *Forbes*, *AdWeek*, and *CIO.*

Michael is the other author of the Amazon #1 bestseller *Crawl, Walk, Run.*

KENT OLDHAM

Kent Oldham is the Chief Operating Officer at InfoTrust, a global privacy-centric digital analytics solutions company. Prior to joining InfoTrust, Kent spent thirty years at Procter & Gamble and his career included leading privacy and security work across 1,000+ sites at the enterprise consumer packaged goods company.

As a husband and father of three boys, Kent and his wife Lisa are enjoying watching each son navigate a different life stage (working, in college, and in high school).

CONTRIBUTORS

CHRIS VAUGHAN

Chris Vaughan is the Director of Strategy at InfoTrust, working with his team to develop rock-solid strategic plans that ensure the company remains the leader in privacy-centric analytics solutions.

Prior to this role, Chris served as InfoTrust's Head of Vertical for CPG, FMCG, and Multi-Brand partners, where he helped the world's largest and most recognizable brands develop, deploy, and measure their digital analytics strategies. Throughout his career, Chris has influenced the digital analytics architectures, data collection methodologies, and insights for thousands of websites and mobile apps around the world.

As a husband and father of three girls, Chris enjoys spending time with his family, working out, and traveling (especially to the Caribbean).

PAM CASTRICONE

Pam Castricone is Head of Data Science at InfoTrust. She helps e-commerce retailers and CPG organizations uncover greater insights and value from their data assets. Specializing in statistical and machine learning models, she applies these advanced analytical techniques to drive better ROI for her clients. As a Google Cloud Certified Professional Data Engineer, Pam also helps her clients productionalize their models in the cloud to drive long-term usability and success.

Pam is also an adjunct professor at the University of Cincinnati's Lindner College of Business, where she teaches a graduate-level course on digital analytics. When she isn't analyzing data, Pam enjoys reading, the arts, and going out for brunch.

TYLER BLATT

In his eight years at InfoTrust, Tyler has brought the concept of full-stack developer to the analytics and marketing tag world. Starting with tag implementation and finishing with data warehouse creation, he has covered the full scope of the analytics data life cycle. He is currently on the strategy team, where he uses his industry experience to determine the best way to adapt to the changing market.

MELANIE BOWLES

Melanie Bowles has been in the digital space for over ten years working on both the agency side and client side. She has been involved with the development of digital and optimization strategies for both SMBs and Fortune 500 companies across industries. Specializing in digital transformation, Melanie has been a catalyst for helping businesses increase traffic, improve customer experience, and increase conversions and revenue. Melanie is currently an Industry Team Lead at InfoTrust, where she partners with multifunctional teams to define analytics strategy, analyze data, and evaluate the business impact of digital experiences for financial, automotive, and B2B verticals.

PETER CROFUT

Peter Crofut is the Director of Partnerships at InfoTrust overseeing the company's partnership with Google. As Google's former Chief Platforms Evangelist, he partnered with the C-Suite of Google's largest brands to accelerate their digital display, data, and analytics transformations.

Peter is recognized as a pioneer and expert in the intersection of data analytics, cloud, and display platform technologies. His thought leadership has been published in *Forbes* and Think with Google; he also guest lectures at some of the world's top business schools and industry forums.

COURTNEY FENSTERMAKER

Courtney is an Industry Team Lead for InfoTrust's Direct-to-Consumer digital analytics team. Starting her career in digital marketing consulting, she brings a strategic, "big-picture" perspective of how our clients can best leverage their data for marketing activation and insight generation. Since then, Courtney has focused her career on first-party data strategies and privacy-centric digital analytics practices to help retail and e-commerce organizations build a genuine and trusting connection with their customers.

Outside of InfoTrust, Courtney is also passionate about her involvement in the Digital Analytics Association (DAA), where she sits in key roles on the Privacy and Ethics Committee and the Implementation Task Force, and acts as a Women in Analytics (WIA) mentor. In her free time, she loves attending a game at her local AAA baseball stadium or checking out the newest restaurants in the area with her husband.

TOM LUNDIN

Tom is the Industry Team Lead for InfoTrust's Consumer Packaged Goods team. Working with a team of talented analysts from five countries and three continents, the group leads the digital analytics strategy and implementations for some of the world's largest organizations. He has over fifteen years of experience in the digital analytics industry and enjoys the daily challenge of adapting the ever-changing landscape of digital analytics tools to each company's unique organizational structure and needs, all with an eye to the critical importance of privacy and global consumer data regulations.

When away from his desk, you'll usually find Tom outside with his family, exploring the natural beauty that Pennsylvania has to offer on a bike ride, paddling down a stream, or hiking through the woods.

JAMES LOVE

James is the Industry Team Lead for InfoTrust's Healthcare & Fitness digital analytics team. He's been at InfoTrust for over ten years, starting as a marketing intern out of the University of Cincinnati. Other previous roles include the Advertising Manager prior to InfoTrust's transition to a full-time analytics-exclusive company. In addition to leading an industry team of rock star analysts, James works with some of the largest organizations in the world, helping them advance their digital analytics maturity in a forward-thinking and strategic manner.

Outside of work, James enjoys attending Cincinnati Bearcats football and basketball games, and spending quality time with his beautiful wife and dogs.

KRISTI MORIN

Kristi is an Industry Team Lead for InfoTrust's Direct-to-Consumer digital analytics team. She has been a consultant in the marketing analytics field for over fifteen years with experience spanning multiple vertices including online, print, B2B, and DTRV. Her career fulfillment comes from helping to support her retail clients that have digital storefronts to plan and execute strong analytic strategies that become foundational to informing their general business and marketing optimization decision-making.

Outside of InfoTrust, Kristi is a proud mom of two beautiful little girls. And because two kids aren't enough to keep her busy on the weekends, she is also the founder and President of a local 501(c)(3) nonprofit organization that organizes social activities for other working moms in her local area to meet and mingle with each other. If she ever does opt for a career change, it will definitely be to pursue her passion for event planning!

ACKNOWLEDGMENTS

LUCAS LONG

Thank you to all of my friends and family for their unwavering support in whatever I decide to commit my time and effort to.

I'd like to thank my coauthors—Michael, Alex, and Kent—for their time and dedication to this project. Sessions of kicking around ideas and making sense of the various technical and regulatory changes have helped in clarifying my opinions and understanding tremendously.

Thank you to all of my wonderful colleagues at InfoTrust. The depth of knowledge across so many disciplines that you all have never ceases to amaze me. Being able to learn from you every day has led directly to many of the strategies and recommendations covered in this book.

Thank you finally to all of the amazing clients and partners that I have the pleasure of working with on a regular basis. It is your questions and needs that keep the job fun and exciting. By allowing me to explore these needs with you, you guide my curiosity and provide the motivation to deeply understand these topics to be able to teach and provide leadership more effectively. This book and the ideas that fill it would not be possible if not for you all.

MICHAEL LOBAN

I would like to acknowledge the following people:

My parents, who made the decision to immigrate to the United States and give me the opportunity for a better future. Their support has allowed me to pursue my passions, including this book.

My aunt and uncle, who always treated me as their second son and instilled in me an urge to learn and explore not just in work, but in life.

Alex, Kent, Lucas, and all of our co-contributors, who not only brought their wisdom and ideas to this book but worked relentlessly to put it all together. This would not be possible without their knowledge, expertise, and dedication.

The entire InfoTrust team, who inspire me to grow and be more impactful in my decisions and actions. Your breadth of skills, knowledge, and passion always propels me forward.

Mona Nikhanj, Deane Wagner, Jessica Qaasim, Laurie Kyser, Sharen Phillips, Paul Limbrey, and the entire Google Marketing Platform Partner Team for supporting and growing our partnership.

Neil Hoyne, your book *Converted* is a true inspiration. I am grateful for your friendship and a chance to learn from you, brainstorm different ideas, and partner on interesting projects. Your feedback always expands my thinking.

The InfoTrust advisory board—Jeff Lloyd, Tarek Kamil, Tarita Preston, and Tim Butler—for ongoing guidance and sharing your business acumen to help us grow and recognize possible challenges before they even arise.

Dr. Art Shriberg, for mentoring me through the years and inviting me to contribute to his book, *Practicing Leadership*. I am always deeply touched by your continued support and inspiration.

Abie Ingber, for friendship, mentorship, and living a life of service. You inspire me to be a better person.

Michael Bernoff, for teaching me how to be a better communicator. The opportunity to learn from you over the past few years has been transformative.

ALEX YASTREBENETSKY

I would like to thank all of our contributors and my coauthors. Thank you for the opportunity to learn from all of you. You are true professionals in all you do and amazing human beings and leaders.

Nothing has changed or influenced my life more than the birth of my three children Ilya, Anna, and Maria. May you always have peaceful sky over your heads.

I want to thank my amazing wife Karina. None of this would be possible without your love and support.

We are finishing this book in a world very different from the world when we started this project. It took a miracle for my parents to get out of war-torn Ukraine in March 2022.

KENT OLDHAM

To my parents Dale and Marilyn Oldham, thank you for giving me the foundation to find my way in the world.

To my wife Lisa, thank you for always being there in the highs and lows of life.

To my three sons Zach, Max, and Clayton, thank you for being the amazing young men you are and for inspiring me to learn every day just to try and stay even with your knowledge.

To everyone at InfoTrust, thank you for being awesome day in and day out.

Printed in Great Britain
by Amazon

18124016R00119